Testimony for Jesus Christ Is The Messiah

The Living Son of God

SENG CHAO

Copyright © 2025 by Seng Chao

ISBN: 978-1-77883-470-7 (Paperback)

978-1-77883-535-3 (Ebook)

All rights reserved. No part of this publication may be reproduced, distributed, or transmitted in any form or by any means, including photocopying, recording, or other electronic or mechanical methods, without the prior written permission of the publisher, except in the case brief quotations embodied in critical reviews and other noncommercial uses permitted by copyright law.

The views expressed in this book are solely those of the author and do not necessarily reflect the views of the publisher, and the publisher hereby disclaims any responsibility for them.

BookSide Press
877-741-8091
www.booksidepress.com
orders@booksidepress.com

Contents

Who Are You, Lord? I Am Your Father.	v
Introduction	1
My Mother's Life	11
Accepted Jesus as Our Savior	15
Migraine Headache	17
I Am Your Father	19
The Temptation	20
The First Power in the Name of Jesus	22
The Insects Left the Front Yard	23
Mice stop biting the house	24
Healing My Thumb	24
What Is Cancer?	26
Healing Cancer for A Black Lady	28
Healing Cancer for Young White Lady	29
Healing the Appendix	30
Cancer Can Move Around and Talk	33
Special Forgiveness for My Bad Neighbor	36
Left My Full-Time Job	37
Miraculous Reunion with My Wife	39
Healing a Man With Stroke	41
Letter from Foucho's Daughter	42
Changing Flight to Sacramento	43
Healing a Hmong Boy	45
Destroyed the Cross in 1999	50
First Case	50
Second Case	51
My House's Mortgage Paid Off Through a Miracle	52
Miracle Lunch With My Wife	53
Healing Cancer	54
Welcome Jesus to Lunch	56
Demons In the Silver Bars and Gold Coins	57

Healing My Food Poison	59
Leading an Old friend to Accept Jesus Christ	59
Demon Spirit Slept with a Young Lady	62
Another Cancer Healed	63
Healing a Lady with Rhino Horn and Mental Illness	65
Empty Wheelchair for Older Man	68
A 4 year old girl who see spirits.	70
A man healed from seizure	71
My testimonies of blessings	71
The Church	73
Church Building	76
Time Frame	78
Pastor Dawin Cranor, Paul Seng Chao, Fay Chao dress in Lao clothes.	82

Who Are You, Lord? I Am Your Father.

Jesus Christ is the Messiah as same Buddha have claimed the Mahesima, **Maitreya** or **Messiah.** Jesus Christ is the same healer today as over 2000 years ago and forever. The mental illness, cancers, and other infirmities are the work of demonizes spirits.

God the father and Jesus Christ are still working every second to hear our cries, our problems, and give peace and love to all who ask and follow his commandments, He will answer our prayers. For God the father and Jesus Christ never change, always the same. God gives us Jesus: He is the way to peace and life eternal. John 5:17

"For God so loved the world, that He gave his only begotten Son, that whosoever believeth in Him shall not perish, but have everlasting life.

For God sent not his Son into the world to condemn the world; but that the world through him might be saved. **John 3:16-17** KJV.

Peter answered them, "All of you must turn to God and change the way you think and act, and each of you must be baptized in the name of Jesus Christ so that your sins will be forgiven. Then you will receive the Holy Spirit as a gift. 39 This promise belongs to you and to your children and to everyone who is far away. It belongs to everyone who worships the Lord our God." Acts 2:38

Introduction

My name is **Seng Loung Chao (Paul)** from a small country called **Laos,** in Southeast Asia in 1960. Lao was in a Civil War and then Laos was drag in to Vietnam War and whole country fell into the hands of the Lao Communists which was supported by North Vietnam in 1975. For years the food was in shortage, the country was in turmoil and the people were in fear. We didn't know what was going to happen in next second. Will we live or will we be the next one to die? The government was unstable and there was no justice anywhere in the country. There were corruptions and crimes in every neighborhood. If the communists discover our community, they will kill every man and women and children. They would say that we sympathize with the United States Government. So we had to escape our country, left our home and everything behind or we would be killed. Many soldiers or ex-government workers were captured by the Communists and sent to the prison camp and some killed. So, we fled our beloved country to Thailand for safety.

This book is a testimony about Jesus Christ around the globe between God's Kingdom and demonic kingdom, between Asian world and Western world. I had passed through the demonic kingdom which is different from the Western world. I came from a small country called Laos, but my ancestors were from a small tribe called Yao in China. We had carried our traditions for thousands of years without anyone telling us to change and our ancestors had never changed their traditions, but thank God for sending His Son, Jesus Christ to me, opens my eyes, and the Holy Spirit of God gave me the understanding.

For some Asian women who are with babies in their wombs, the shamans call the ancestral spirits to protect the babies with good health. After the babies are born, the shamans come back to them, collect the vows, and dedicate the babies to the spirits called **TIM MIENH KUV,** to register in to spirit kingdom or to be membership of spirit family. This part is very danger. then make the second vow to protect the babies for growing up with good health, but the babies always get sick and become handicaps all the time, and even death, but still need to pay for the vows and make sure spirits look after them until 12 years old. How do we know that the spirit, we never seen to be trust, good or bad, as we know, today all spirits or demonic are the killer or murderers. The non-Christians in America continue the same practice in the U.S and around the globe. Let think, why the west always advances in many hi-tech or modern technologies, but the Asian east always copies then make better never created somethings new. Because Asian mind was block by God. God know, most Asian people were dedicated to spirits, it cause our mind to polluted mind, unthinkable, call animal mind like Chinese zodiac like animals year, to make people believe to born in year of dragon, or ox or rats so to people like animal, Satan try to find many ways to make your mind like animal, think like animal, act like animal. like King Nebuchadnezzar unable to think just eat grass for 7 years. When God open his mind then he became human. Dan 4:32-34. When idols come to the land, trouble follow like famine, chaos in politic, economies, and turmoil. All come along with it. Whatever we worship to put our mind like what we worship so may nation just worship nature like rock, trees, Buddha, ancestor spirits like my ancestor did. Humans want to worship something can see by their eyes. Satan Just want to change people's mind into animal mind, to pollute our mind to confuse for us unable to communicate to God, for us unable to communicate to God directly. Satan try so many ways to block our ways to communicate directly to God in pray or in natural or spiritual way, whatever we see, then worship it.

My name is Seng Loung Chao. Seng Means to tie, Loung means the dragon. So, my name is **tie to dragon** (dragon is spirit). My father thought that it was a good name, but I had still been sicked all my childhood and youth, until God released me from the bondage. If anybody welcomes an ancestral spirit, the other 7 spirits or more follow it without asking permission. (**Matthew 12:45; Luke 11:26**) says that we need to only accept the Spirit of God and The Savior Lord Jesus Christ, God's only begotten Son.

The picture was taken in 1978. Seng Loung Chao (Paul) 21 years old at a Refugee Camp in Thailand, smoked 2 packs of cigarettes a day, and drank all time, sick all time. I thought of committing suicide many times because I lived my youthful life like hell, but God saved my life for a reason and for His Kingdom.

1. After a child is 12 years old, she or he is escaped from the babyhood to the adulthood and pays the vows at this

first stage. This first stage permits 12 spirits to follow the child to the next vow which is called, "**Bietv faatv**" (the transfer of the magical power) and permits the 24 spirits to live with the child.

2. The second stage of vows is called **GUAAX DANG** (the first degree merits the lamp ceremony) which permits the 5 masters or teachers, including the grand spirits, masters, family spirits and 36 spirits to be the bodyguard for the child at this second stage.

3. The third stage is called **DOUC SAI** (second degree merit ceremony hall) call 120 spirits, or bodyguards to protect the man.

4. The fourth stage of vows is called **JAA^ZEQV** (third degree merit ceremony hall) which calls the 60 grand spirits or soldiers to protect the man.

5. Then fifth stage of vow is called **JAA^TAAIX** (promote the grand master merit ceremony hall) calls 60 grand spirits or soldiers to protect the man. That's why the man always smoke opium or use other drugs for healing, Fifth stages. By this time almost over 500 spirits and grand spirits are with the man all the time. They may see them or not, but that's what they believe. It is true or not they just follow this tradition from generation to generation without finding out from wrong to right or from right to wrong path. Like blind generation guide the next blind generation, keep on going until God shows me, Jesus is the only way, the life and the truth. Now, the Thai, Lao, Chinese or Cambodian people believe in Buddhism and Buddha. Asian community do the similar tradition

called: **Buatc** (purification merit ceremony). Some Asian countries have colleges to teach the fasting and purification of Buddha or purification merit ceremony hall.

1. First stage fasting or self-purification (merit purification ceremony) to call **NERN, buotc**. For 5-7 days for 5 vows to stop 5 sins. Fasting to depend on spirits power to release other sins. For any boy in the family must **BUOTC** or **SELF-PURIFY** at one time just for meeting the standard of their tradition, but women don't do anything except supply food for the monks when they pass by every morning to collect the needed, foods and supplies to take back to the temple. Some women volunteer but not demand to be purified. Sins and spirits are the same family.

2. Second stage is called **Siang_naan.** For 2 months or more for stopping 227 sins.

3. Third stage is called **TITV NOIV. TU POR** another stage for life. To be masters in the temple for half of life or for a lifetime, no women come close. But many monks have children in their villages. All these stages, depend on spirits or demonic help to survive. There are only two kingdoms on earth. God's kingdom or spirits' kingdom, we must depend on only one kingdom. So, all Asians depend on spirits, that's all they know. You may travel to Asia like Thailand or Laos and see that almost every family has a small hut in front of the house for spirits to dwell, for burning incenses and bowing down to worship the spirits in the morning. They always said, if we do good things good will return. They never teach the way and the life to heaven.

On the other hand, a little section in the Buddha book says (I am not life, **Maitreya** (same as **Messiah**), or the way, He will come after me, He will take all human sins, and His hand and feet have marks of stamp). Those community do not know who they call or depend on. When the spirits come, sicknesses also come, when you possess spirits, you possess sickness or infirmities. and possess curses. But people do not understand until last minute and it's too late. Asian community, all children must listen to their parents' order, you must obey, you must obey, must, must do it or out of the house because no education to improve their knowledge for knowing the Lord God to be our help. But in Western or American world is a total difference. When women are pregnant, first thing they do is to look for Vitamin to be sure that the mother and baby are in good health. After the baby is born, we make sure that both mother and baby are having enough nutrition, in good health and enough diapers for the baby. And never mess with spirits. Believe in spirits and register to spirits are two totally different subjects.

But to the most of Asian communities everything is ancestral spirits, or family spirits (**ong-taaix**) powerful spirits like Kungfu spirits, master spirits make people jump across the roof top, black magic spirits, trick, nails shooting this can kill someone 5-10 miles away without going to the person, very dark world and people sick all the time, easy way to madness, easy and fast fighting. I have seen them with my own eyes that they jump from this house over to other house by power of spirits. You may notice in every Asian store have little spirits hut inside store for burning incense and some fruit in it for their ancestor spirits which mean all in tire the store, all things have been sacrifice and offer to their spirits. Even, in the front of restaurant also burn to spirits.

When I go and pray for 100 Westerners, most of them are healed, but only 10 out of the 100 Asians may be healed. Those, who are healed, but their sickness always come back again because they do not abide by God's Words, Laws, and the Holy Spirit. Some people go to church and all their sickness are gone, but after they go home the sickness come back again. When I go to some people's homes to pray for them, they are healed, but when I go home their sickness come back again. We must cancel all vows or idols in our life now or ancestor's vow in the past. So many times, the vows from our parents never cancel due to our parent passed away or forgotten or lack of fund. Whatever vow must pay back even time passed by us always forget but the spirits never forgotten.

They go to doctors and the doctors are unable to find out what is wrong, but when they come home, they are sick again. That's what happen to my wife who was sick for years until doctor gave up and refer her to apply for Supplemental Security Income, but she refused to go because the Supplemental Security Income or SSI will not solve the problem until we find out the whole solution. Demonic spirits are the real cause of sickness. That's why a lot of Asians accept the Lord and slide back to spirits easier than Westerners. Asian are very hard to grow their faith because the spirits control them or surround them from the babyhood. Even when they come to church and accept the Lord Jesus with their mouths, the evil spirits keep on pulling them down and easier being down. Many times, parents made vows to the spirits while kids in college or away from home. Usually, they dedicate their children's date of birth, including hour of the day, month and year to the spirits. That's why you always see the timetable in Chinese restaurant or calendar, like horoscope. You might be born in the year of monkey, horse, tiger and so on…, they make egg standing or water turn in different color by power of spirits. Many times, children know nothing or what parents did. Sometimes, parents put spirits in the bracelet with Buddha idol, then send kid to college in America. When children are sick, they can't find answers, and the doctors have no answers, either.

When Asian people decide to follow God and Jesus Christ and Holy Spirit.

What should they do?

1. They must cancel all vows to any spirits, generation curse or master spirits. They need to cancel the family spirits, name by name, then accept Jesus Christ to be their Master and be baptized in the name of Jesus Christ. Fast and pray for days until God answers their prayers. Make sure you really know Jesus Christ and accept Him in your heart like fire or electric. Ask for blood of Jesus and hedge it around our lives all the time (Acts 3:38-39, Eph 6:12-20).

2. Burn all antiques such as clothes, objects, materials, and equipment that have been used for worshiping the spirits because they symbolize the statute of dragon, snake and so on. The pictures of ancestors that have incenses and been used for worshipping the spirits before. Or any idols must be burned in fire. If any idol temple, it must be burned down because God calls that place a defiled or dirty spot. God never come down to that place, if too many temples in the country, the whole country will be in chaos or curse of God.

3. Fast and pray until Holy Spirits sanctify them and back to God 100% or they will never escape because their vows are so powerful in spirits kingdom. I am not talking about salvation. That is between you and God. While you are on earth, you must be happy and peaceful.

4. Stay away from the spirits, family of non-believers, old friends because I have seen many Asian pastors graduated from the Bible college and pastoring in church for years, later divorced their wives and denied the Lord Jesus and married other women and never go to church again. Some go back to worship old ancestors again or back to be shaman again. Outside look like they are full of righteousness, but their inside is still possessed by spirits, demons and shamanism. If any person really receives Jesus, sanctify by the Holy Spirit, he/she never goes back to any other religion again. I was in the second stage, hook into 24 spirits by my father even I didn't live with him, but he got all my information and put me in the 24 spirits. So, I must fast and pray for 40 days twice to make sure that all the spirits have nothing to do with me. I was a 100% sinner, but now, I belong to the Living God Jesus Christ 100% and not of this world.

My wife and I always fighting, we didn't know what it cause. Sometime, just small thing soon became huge problem. We try to divorce but no chance, but if we don't see each other, it's seeming we love each other. I keep pray ask God. Then God show me the generation antiques, which she got it from her parents. She never talked about it. Before my wife always mad or complain something after coming from work and never happy. She mad all time. After God reveal to me the generation gods, the silver coins and silver bar, I took them outside the house burn in fire. Say nothing until evening, she came home smile and most happy, she cooks and ate together, no fight, problem. All problem vanishes by itself. Now, I know all the cause is spirits are in the silver coins and silver bar or gold coins. Read the book Isaiah 44:6-23. Judge chap 19 to 21. Confusion in the country and similar War in Asia. Asia countries full of idols, temples, possess the curse of God, that's why chaos, fighting, famine, poverties around the region. I had cancel all my past from my parent's vow or dedicated to spirits or idols or any master spirits then I felt something like heavy burden yoke released from my body then my body so light at that moment my body seems no more sickness but exciting, peace, enjoy life, can't explain the peace within me, all I can tell was transforming new life like reborn again.

My Mother's Life

My mother and father have many children after many years in marriage. The war broke out in the country between North and South Vietnam, when the North Vietnam was unable to go to South because of the US Army and South Vietnam are blocking them in the middle, then North made a short cut through Laos and Laos was dragged in the war because of the Ho Chi Minh Trail. The war broke-out in our village, the soldiers used our house as fighting ground. One morning, the communist was shooting, and bullets came into the house while my grandmother was holding my older brother who was about 2 years old. The bullets shot through the chest of the baby and cut off half nose of my grandmother. The baby died in her arms and my family were crying, mourning and wailing for months. The dead bodies were all over the village. My father and my oldest sister and some villagers must bury the dead. The fear and trauma were full in every house. My other brother-Kao died only a few months after that. A year later my other brother Ousengx died from pestilences. Two more years later, my other sister-Naitong died in sickness, too. Five more years later, my other sister-Chio died. My father always went out for business, returned home less and less.

Finally, my father found another lady and divorced my mother. My mother lost 5 children. Only my two sisters, my mother and I survived. My mother went to her family after the completion of the divorce. We lived in peace with my mother's family for many years until the war came to her family's province. My mother, then developed a mental problem suddenly without notice and no one knew the cause, but many believed that the influence of demonic spirits made her became manic depression. Some thought that it was a traumatic disorder, but they were not sure. Her life changed suddenly, and she completely became a different person. She often left our home to stay in the cemetery. When we found her in the cemetery, we asked her why she came to the cemetery, and she always answered that she was looking for her children. We knew she loved her children very much. Her mind always stayed with her dead children. She always moved from village to village, always moved, had hallucination and was talking to the spirits.

The country was a dangerous place for our family, especially her due to her insanity. She refused to return home. Communication was difficult with her because she was deaf in both ears. She could not hear us unless we were within 2 feet from her, but she heard the spirits or demons clearly. We had to find a way to heal her, and hundreds of shamans came to our home and prayed for her, but she was worse and worse. The shamans always told us to sacrifice cows, chickens, ducks and goats to spirits and we did every time. We had to spend all of our money away, but she was not healed. She got worst. We took her to a Buddha temple for healing, but the result was the same, and it did not help. Then, we took her to a small medical clinic, then a hospital and even the biggest mental hospital, but none of them could help her.

By this time our money had been depleted and the hope for a better future was gone. Our family cried day and night for a long time and eventually our family members became violent due to our dear mother's mental illness. She was the only mother, and we loved her. Her problems were too much for my father and he ended up divorcing her. I was 1 year old at the time, and I never saw my father and have not heard from him ever since. Sometimes, I looked at the sky and asked angels to see whether any of them had seen my father, but none of say anything. I needed help because my mother was poor and lived in a terrible life. I tried to find help, but there was no answer to my effort. We lost the war and the whole Laos was taken over by the Lao Communists in 1975. Whoever worked for the US Government, or the Royal Lao Government had to leave the country for safety. So, we escaped to Thailand as refugees. We had to adjust to a new life in the camp for more than 4½ years.

In the refugee camp, life was horrible. There was no electricity and no furniture. Each family lived in a 100-square-foot room. The room had no beds, and we had to sleep on the floor. The kitchen was in the living rooms, too. Later, I served as a Food Control Officer and by doing so, I was able to marry my wife in Thailand, and we have had 2 boys and a girl now. I had more freedom and was able to move to a bigger house. The new house was 200 square feet, and I was able to get in and out of the camp easier than other people. Even with the new freedom, it still did not help my mother's situation. She was still crying, yelling, talking to herself, growing mad most of the days and nights. This kept everyone up and no one was able to sleep at night.

The neighbors grew angry and so mad and asked me to put my mother outside the camp. I could not do so because she was the only mother that I have ever had. I just could not do such a thing to her. Not long after that the United States Embassy came to the camp and started to register those who wanted to go the United States of America to start a new life. I used to work for USAID in Laos and was eligible to register for going to the United States. My family and I left the camp and entered the USA for a new life in 1980. This new life in the USA was very different from Thailand and Laos. Even with this long move it still did not change the condition of my mother because her illness was still with her.

We landed in Seattle, Washington. The city was beautiful, full of luxurious modern technology and the homes were far more advanced than the homes in Laos. We still carried the burden of the war with us to our new home. There were no shamans in the United States. We tried to look for shamans as in the old countries but could not find one at first. We found someone later, but it seemed to have no help. Later the shamans referred my mother to Jesus Christ that He might be able to help her. This was the first time I heard a shaman refer her to Jesus Christ for help. I, then had some questions in my mind, "Who is Jesus? Where does He live? What does He look like? What kinds of food he eats? And what kind of house does he lives in? The reason I had those questions was because I had heard people talk about Jesus as Yesu in Laos and Thailand, but no one really told me who He was or what exactly He would be able to do.

I took my mother from county to county from hospital to hospital in search of a way to heal her, but no one and nothing could help. Not even one person could slow down the anger she developed from her mental disabilities. Many times, she went to the store and took whatever she wanted and no one would stop her. She took foods, clothes, and knives. She ended up hurting somebody, but the police could not stop her and just left her alone. When a person is possessed by demonic spirits, the power of the spirit controls that person's thoughts and action, including murdering others, or spirits control person where to go, too. **Matthew 8:28.** When my mother was fine, she always put me in her arms and laps from my birth to childhood. Sometimes, I asked myself, why it happens to this poor mother of mine this way, one of the most humble person you would ever met, and in the past she was live in hell. I shed my tears in my early life for her. I feel the love and care of her heart. I look at her face, she is my comforter and my shelter.

Accepted Jesus as Our Savior

One day in 1982, a man came to me and asked, "Do you know Jesus?" He said that Jesus would be able to help my mother's situation. If I accepted Jesus and believed in him, and welcomed him into my life, then my mother's problem would be solved. It sounded like a joke, and it was impossible to me that Jesus would take care of her problem because she had been to too many hospitals, taking so much medication and prayers without result. I thought for a moment. Where does Jesus live? When I went to the doctor, I would see Him face to face and if I went to Buddha, he would sit in front of me or standing taller than a house. Buddha was all over Asia, full of almost every high mountain. Buddha was unable to help, nor the doctors. I did not see Jesus in person. How this Jesus would be able to help. It seemed almost impossible to get the answer for her conditions. I tried hard but found no answer or help. So, I made an appointment to meet with the church elders and pastor and invited them to my home for a try. They came to our home, but I didn't see Jesus come with them. Who Jesus is? I kept on thinking how could this be possible. They started service and burned all the ornaments that were used for worshipping the ancestors and spirits. They threw everything into the fire and burned them. Then my whole family accepted the Lord Jesus Christ as our Savior in late 1982. It was a cold winter, and I didn't remember the date, but we began learning how to sing hymns and how to pray to the Lord God. We prayed daily for a while, then my mother stopped talking to herself and started sleeping during the day and night. The same medication that did not work before but worked now. Finally, my whole family found peace and was able to rest. Our family was at peace and my mother was able to recognize her children and grandchildren, too.

From left to right: My son Roger, Nai,, Cindy Saechao and my mother, Mueycho Saechao. She was happy with her grandchildren after she was healed from the mental illness.

My mother's mental illness was healed by Jesus Christ, and she lived a happy life until she had her heart attack and passed away on Dec 25, 2003. She was 84 years old and died in peace. She finally went with the Lord with her last breath. After she got healed from her mental illness in 1983, I got a chance to wander around from town to town to visit friends and do something fun. I no longer had to look after my mother. I was able to go to bars at night, drinking with my friends, enjoying worldly life and stayed late into the night. Soon I stopped going to church. I only went to church because Jesus Christ was my mother's God. Since she got better, I ignored what God did for her. Soon, I forgot what He has done for her, I owed a lot of thanks to the Living God, but I forget Him all. It seemed that God was no longer important to me. I thought just like after we healed and come back from hospital then we don't have to go back to hospital again, but we must pray and communication to God every day. This is all of human being's attitudes and error.

Migraine Headache

I started drinking in 1983 and did not get enough sleep, and migraine headache started. I was unable to sleep at night, eat, or open my eyes at home. In many occasions, I closed my eyes and fell asleep at work. I took sick leave constantly and used up all my vacation. And worst of all, I lost my job in Seattle, Washington, then move to California to look for healing, but nothing healed me. I took different kind of medications, visited different doctors, but none of them could do any good. I tried all kinds of medicines from different countries such as herbs, Marsha and even codeine # 3 which contains opiate, but they were useless.

Due to the codeine, I took, and I became an opiate addictive and craved for it more and more. It felt like if I smoke the opium, I will get better, but it did not help, either. Finally, I realized that I had nothing left except to return to Jesus Christ the Lord for help. I prayed to Him, but no response. I went to many pastors, and they prayed for me, too, but the result was the same. Now my faith came into question. I was questioning where Jesus Christ was, how could I find Him, and how could I get the answer? Is this the real Jesus? or was this just another religion? Those pastors kept on talking about Jesus and how He helped my mother's problems. I, then started to ask some questions like where is He, how can I find Him or when He would answer me? I read the Bible, but it seemed like only some stories from the old days.

The Bible said, Jesus healed the blind, forgave transgressors, and so on (Luke 4:18-19), but they seemed like only some stories until one day I was rushed to the emergency room in the hospital. The doctors injected me a lot of morphine for the pain, but it did not help at all. I was crying, yelling for the doctor, rolling around and around, and they had to tie me down on the hospital bed. I could not move, could not get up and then I prayed. "I am confessing my sins to you, my Lord Jesus Christ. Please take me out of the turmoil, give me freedom, free me from the responsibility of looking after my mother who was mentally disabled by healing her, you brought me here to serve you, but I have not done so. I was so happy to be free and wasting my time by partying. So now, I am asking you to, please forgive me and free me again. If you are the resurrected God and alive, come to me, talk to me and heal me. I will go around the world, telling the whole world that you are the living God. I promised to keep my words as I spoke today, and will you also keep your words as they are in the heaven?" Suddenly, something happened, the big fan blew from the ceiling down on me in the hospital bed, electric rained like fire and shocked my whole body, I was crying even more because of the sins, the quilt within me like the coldest ice and fire mix together within my body. At that moment, the pain was gone, total healing took place, right after the Lord God touched me. Now I am a free man. I told my wife I'm ok now, let's go home. She went to tell the nurse, but the doctor did not know.

The doctor pushed me in to the surgery room and tried to perform a surgery on me, but I told him I was healed. The surgeon asked, "Are you sure?" I answered, "Very sure. God came to me a moment ago. I want to go home, here is not fun, let me go please." The surgeon said again, "You will go home if you are sure OK, but I think you are very scared of the surgery, aren't you?" I replied, "I'm sure, God came and healed me, yes, yes, I am healed." The surgeon said, "If the real God healed you, then go home." The doctor could not believe it at first, but finally believed me, and released me to go home. I am the first generation to call on the name of Jesus Christ the Savior the living God. It's hard to explanation what God look like and how His power be compared to human ability. Today I go to around the world tell the people Jesus Christ is The Messiah, the living Son of God. Specially, I go to highlanders or mountain people to tell, and lead come to **Jesus Christ is The Messiah.** Specially, in Asia continent.

I Am Your Father

After I was healed and came home from the hospital in 1992, I kept on praising the Lord every day and every night. The Lord always came to me just like the time in the hospital. I began to witness about God's healing, how God healed me. Then people ask me, what kind of God is that came like fire and water as you have said? **Mat 3:11** (NIV). Now more and more people came and ask me to pray for their healing; many sick people have been healed. I prayed to God Day after day, one day, I went to Benny Hinn crusade service in Long Beach, California. While the service was going for about two hours, I felt somebody hold on to me like father hold unto his son. I asked, *"Who are you, Lord?" "I am your father." He answered. I asked again, "Who are you, Lord?" Then the voice spoke to me very clearly within my heart that, "I am your father, whom you have been looking for a long time, I am your father." I said, "Please hold me forever Lord."* He answered again, "Yes, I will." I, then totally felt that He was inside me, in a joint union within me, the fear in me for a long time quickly disappeared and all my sickness were gone. My mental problems were like my mother's for a long, but I knew how to control it now. The truth is I have handled my mother's situation long enough to transfer all her problems to me or my whole family. At that moment, *I was totally transfigured into a new body. I felt much lighter. Now I can fly into the sky, joy, peace within me.* He is my father forever and in me John 14:23. Since that day, I have not taken any more medication or go to doctor again until today.

Later, I learned that the more medication I took, the more sickness came to my body because medication always heals one thing and kills something else in my body. The more doctor I see, the more my eyes focus on to doctor, every day, I thought that the doctor or medication was my help. Now, my eyes are off the doctor and medication, too. So, my mind can focus on God alone. See, most people love God and want to see God with their own eyes. Or see something before they believe like I was, I am just another Thomas the doubted, (John 20:27).

People worship Buddha idols in front of them even Buddha made of cement and made of clay, so they think that the idols can help because they see them with their own eyes, but **our God is the God** that made heaven and earth, and He is bigger than heaven and earth. People will think that He can't come unto our hearts because He is too big to fit in our hearts. God can be anywhere our hearts, the stars, suns belong to Him. Wherever He wants to be, no one can stop Him. Let's think about the complexity of the stars, moon, and the biggest universe. And the complexity of the smallest objects such smallest tiny cells that even the microscope is almost unable to see, but they are all made by God. Human minds are too narrow to understand God. The facts, we don't know real God.

The Temptation

In 1993, I was in a Baptist church. Many of my friends in the congregation did not know about the Holy Spirit. In those days, I came back from Israel and in one Sunday service, I went up to the stage to pray for the congregation, suddenly, the choir fall to the ground, some crying, some laughing, and some praising the Lord God, some speaking in tongue. The power of the Holy Spirit filled the whole church. We knew the power of the Holy Spirit, but we didn't know how to discern the Holy Spirit and how to follow the Power of Holy Spirit. Since that day, some visitors from other churches reported to their congregations that Paul Seng Chao was a cult, out of mind and made the whole church crazy together with him that day. The confusion began at that church. One said one thing and others said other things, some pastors came to me and told me that they wanted me to stop talking about the Holy Spirit and stop teaching about another God the Holy Spirit. They wanted me to just keep on preaching the good news about Jesus Christ the Savior.

If I did not stop and the church would split. I explained that I talked about the Holy Spirit because I was unable to see him in my personal eyes. Yet I could see Jesus in my spiritual eyes. In my understanding, there are three dimensions in the Old Testament: 1) The time of Jehovah God the father, Elohim God, 2) The time of Jesus Christ the Savior, The son of God and 3) The time of Holy Spirit the counselor today. Today is the time of the Holy Spirit's dimension, after Jesus was caught up to heaven. Before the Lord Jesus Christ came into earth, He was still the Holy Spirit Mat 1.18. God is the Spirit. If you worship God, you must worship Him in the Spirit and truth John 4:24. Today, Jesus comes in Spirit realm. We can't see him in our natural eyes. The truth is Jesus already around us every day, day in and day out. Many times, we hear voices inside our hearts, but we can't see him. We should talk, teach, and preach about the Holy Spirit, the Holy Spirit is our helper for ministries to grow, too. (John 4:24, John 14:16-17, John 14:23).

No matter how hard I explained about the Holy Spirit, those pastors did not listen to me and rejected my explanation. So, I separated from them and their congregations. Then, the persecution began within our community, and they turned their back on me because I believe in the Holy Spirit. The price Jesus have paid on the Cross, the shame, shedding the blood and lost all his own family identity,

His family dis-owned Him, but he has been famous in the kingdom of God (Mat 12:46-50).

To know the Lord God, mean to separate from community and religions. Jesus is not religion, but God. There is a huge price I must pay for our faith and what I believe, too. Then our church split into two. One group packed and left the church. but most of them remained stay the church. Confusion arose within our churches, but I kept my confident and focused on God. I knew who I worshipped and trusted.

The First Power in the Name of Jesus

I was a drug counselor in 1993. I had to go to work early but could not sleep because the dog was barking behind the neighbor's backyard all night long. I tried to use my fingers to close my ears, but only for a while, then the fingers slipped off the ears. I put a pillow over my head, but it slipped, too. When I started to fall sleep the noise became bigger and bigger, I still could not sleep. I, then prayed to God for help. I prayed and asked God to help stop the dog from barking, help me now Lord, but no answer from God. So, I was mad and prayed with a loud voice, "In the name of Jesus Christ, I command you dog be in peace and stop barking now, now, now.

Then, I heard the dog woofed and stopped from barking the rest of the night. The dog was in peace all night long. I, then couldn't sleep again because I was wondering why I had prayed for such a long time without result, but when I prayed in the name of "Jesus Christ" it worked. The peace went to the dog and the dog did not even make one more voice again all night long. I, then kept on thinking about the result. How can this be? I, then realized that the name Jesus Christ has been the same yesterday, today, and forever. I need to call on the name of Jesus Christ to stop all the diseases and sicknesses, modern violence of gangs and burglars. I should have called the name of Jesus for all my needs long time ago. I, then fell asleep. I have learned a lesson that the power of the Name of Jesus Christ is the highest name above all names, every knee shall bow, and every tongue shall confess His name (Phi 2:10, Isaiah 45.23).

The Insects Left the Front Yard

One early morning in 1993, I was ready to go to work, there were thousands and thousands of black caterpillars in front of my home, I called my family to help me put the insects away, we sprayed the insects killer on them, but in the afternoon when I came home from work, I saw that they were still there and more than double already. We put hot water on them, but soon the hot water was gone without killing them. That night, I used a flash-light to shine to the yard and I saw that they were all there with green eyes. They were so scared of the light and crawled up on the wall of the house or fence, and wherever they could go. For about 3 days, we tried many ways to get rid of them without result. So, I remember about my prayer in the name of Jesus Christ that put the dog in peace, and it slept all night long. I, then prayed along the yard, anointed the olive oil and sanctified the yard. I prayed and commanded all the insects out of my home in the name of Jesus Christ, you all insects get out here now, now, and go now! After that I went to work early in the morning and I came home in the afternoon, I saw that hundreds of small black birds came to pick, dig, and eat all the insects away. None of them left after that day, not one left. Thus, we must pray and command all the problems in the name of Jesus, but we have to cooperate with the Lord God and use the prayer at the right time and right place. Then, all things are possible with God (Mat 19:26).

Mice stop biting the house

One night in 1993, some small mice were biting the house all night long, and I was unable to sleep. I put some rat killer, but it did not help. I prayed with banging on the wall around the house to command them in the name of Jesus, but my voice and banging were not loud enough. The sound and noise were too low, and it did not work. Finally, I prayed with a loud voice and commanded the mice in the name of Jesus Christ, that you all mice go out of my house now, now, now! All the mice and rats heard my prayer with a loud voice and madness from every corner of the house, every place, even from the top of the house. I also went outside and put the olive oil around the house and prayed, then closed the doors. After that day, no more mice and insects came to the house until the day I sold it.

Healing My Thumb

During the time I was a drug counselor in 1994, I always used the pen to write and used computer for work every day. One day, I felt my thumb was painful, unable to write or pick up anything. I dropped even small objects, too. The doctor gave me many pain killers, but they did not help me. The doctor suggested a surgery to cut the front part of the vein off so my thumb might lose the tension and move freely back and forth, but I was afraid that after the surgery my thumb might fell backward, and I might have to live my whole life like that. I didn't want my thumb to be like that forever. I told the doctor, and the doctor said that if it happened that way, I had to live like that for the rest of my life. Now the decision to have a surgery on my thumb was mine alone. I either had a surgery or let it go. The thumb kept on bothering me every day and I was unable to work smoothly. I am praying almost every day but no result. I had no choice but set an appointment for a surgery about 3 weeks later. While I was waiting for my thumb surgery, I heard that the healing service will come to the town and I told my doctor that if my thumb was healed by God, then I might have to cancel the surgery appointment. The doctor laughed at me in the shameful way, but I went to the healing service, and I felt the power of Holy Spirit came upon me, but no healing at that place yet. I was wondering for about a week whether my thumb might be healed from the healing, or I might have to have a surgery.

In a Sunday service, I was frustrated that my thumb was not healed. But a lady came to me and ask for healing prayer for her thumb, too. I looked at her thumb and it was the same thumb as mine which in pain for a long time. I, then asked her, "How long has your thumb in pain like this?" She answered, "More than 2 years now." I, then thought for a moment that God had not healed my thumb, how could I help this lady's thumb, but I did not tell her. I held my peace inside without speaking. I, then put my hand on her and I prayed with madness, "In the name of Jesus Christ of Nazareth, you the thumb pain go away now, now, now, for 3 times. You must go now. Now. Now now!"

Then, I felt something like water flow from my hand out with power straight to that lady's thumb. At that moment that lady yelled and proclaimed, **"I am healed, I am healed now! See, see, my thumb can move freely now."** Suddenly, I felt my thumb was also healed at the same time. My thumb could move freely like hers. Now I have learned a lesson from the Bible that if 2 or 3 of you are together in my name, I am there during you, whatsoever you bind on earth will be bound in heaven. Whatsoever you loose on earth will be loosed in heaven (**Mat 18:18-20**). The more people gather the more power of God is in their midst.

Seng Chao

What Is Cancer?

While I was a young boy in 1958, my mother and father got divorced, I always stayed with only my brother-in-law who married to my older sister. He was dear to me like my father and my real brother. He always shared the food with me and my family when we were in need and gave money to me when I needed it. We were staying together for almost 30 years, then one day, the doctor found out that he had cancer and it was dangerous to his life. I asked the doctor, "What is cancer?" The doctor smiled and said simply that it could be the Hepatitis B. I asked again, "What is Hepatitis B? How serious can it be?" The doctor said that it was so serious, and my brother-in-law had only about 2-3 months to live. I was so shocked and asked the doctor again, "What is cancer?" Is there any medication that can cure this disease?" The doctor replied, "No. No cure for it, ever since I have been a doctor. If it has, we will do for him before you ask." I was so sad and said to myself, "How can I lose my dearest brother in-law who is also my best friend I have ever had? He is a thousand times better than my biological father. He never made me mad. During the time of needs he was always there to help me and my family. He always walked ahead, and I followed behind him.

My heart was depending on him as my shield. Now I am about to lose my hope and my shield, I don't know what to say and do now. I had to cry every day until the time he passed away. I cried too much that I could not really stand because my heart was with emptiness until one day the Lord God came to me and filled my heart with the Holy Spirit. Now, I can feel the Lord's presence everywhere and every day, but it is a different way with the Lord God. I have learned from the Lord God that cancers are real demonic spirit influences in our human life. The doctors can find some ways to cure diseases, but if it comes to the demonic spirit, then they cannot find any kind of medication for healing it. However, after years of praying for people's healing from sicknesses, I started to understand how to pray for the healing from cancer, too. If I knew about this kind of prayer early, I would be able to help my brother in-law and other cousins because they were all died from cancer. First, I thought why all my cousins died from cancer.

Later, I learned that all my cousins had involved with worshipping the demonic spirits and worship the natures before they died, but other races that do not worship demons also die from cancer, too? One day, God revealed to me and I understood the revelation of God that all the human beings have uncontrolled temper and madness which is the highway for the demons to come into human life. After the demons' spirits are in our human life, then there are more madness, resentments, violence, killings, suicides, high emotion, and unforgiveness. All the mental illness, murdering, killings, homicide and assassination are involved with the demonic spirits, no matter what background is, Christianity, Islam or Buddha, any person who serve God or serve demonic spirits. One of my close cousins had been kidnapped since his babyhood and he did not see his parents at all. One day, he found out that his mother was in a village and he went back to look for her, but she was not there. She had died and was buried in the cemetery. He went to the tomb and burned incense, cried and bowed down to the tomb, then went home. He got so sick and went to the doctor. The doctor told him that he had cancer overnight, nothing they could do for him, and he died within that month. See, the demonic spirits are waiting for the right time and opportunity to come into human life like the way they entered my cousin at the tomb. Cancers control the physical. Again, spirits do not have cousins but to kill all. (Gen 4:5-8. Psa 37:8, Pro 15:18).

Healing Cancer for A Black Lady

In 1994, a black lady friend whom I always called her my sister Jackson. She came to me and asked, "Could you go with me to help a dear lady with cancer? The doctor gave her 2 more months to live. Can you go and pray for her?" I replied, "Yes, I will go if you tell me the place where we can meet." She did tell me everything and made an appointment with me. When the appointment time came, Sister Jackson, my wife and I went together to pray for the black lady. Upon our arrival at the black lady's home, I saw that she was hooked up with oxygen in her nose and the oxygen line was stretching all along her home. As soon as I saw her, something came to my mind. No, no way you can heal her. I was thinking in my mind for a moment that I am not a healer, but Jesus is. I am nothing, but Jesus is everything and the only healer.

The Lord Jesus Christ died on the Cross and He is the healer. Everywhere I go, I go for the name of Jesus only. For I am nothing. I must think like this all time. So, we gathered our group around the black lady, then the Holy Spirit revealed to me that she had madness and resentment in her and her family. Before I prayed, I told her that she was carrying her family's sins. There were times that she had too much madness and carry someone's wrongdoing that it became cancer. Then, she confessed about her son who was in and out of the jail for his whole life. She kept on losing her money for him year after year for many years, but he had never changed. He was even got worst from bad.

After her confession, I got close to her big and tall body, then prayed for her. Suddenly, the power of the Holy Spirit came upon her, and she fell to the ground for a while, then stood up and felt the power of God upon her. About a week later, she went to the doctor for a checkup and found out that her cancer was gone. The doctor asked to see what had happened since last visit and she told the doctor about the healing prayer. The doctor, then told her that her cancer was healed and it was ready for her to go back to work again, then she did even she had already withdrawn all her pension from her job during her illness. She went back to work again, but her cancer had never return and she lived for decades after the healing. All things were upside-down, and her cancer was healed because of the name of Jesus Christ the Savior, the healer for all.

Healing Cancer for Young White Lady

In 1994, Sister Jackson saw God did something to last lady, then she called me to go and pray for another lady who was white. This white lady's diagnosis and symptom were about the same as the last black lady. She was lying in bed and waiting to die within about a month according to her doctors. However, her husband refused to let us in to the house to pray for her. We stayed outside and prayed that God opened the husband's heart and let us into their home. Finally, God opened his heart, and he let us in. As soon as we got in, we prayed for her while her husband was standing on her side, watching us with unhappiness. After we finished praying, she stood up and walked around the home, declaring that she was healed. She said that she couldn't walk for months, lost her voice already, but now she was slowly walking and talking again.

The lady received a total healing and went back to school and her full-time job after only a few weeks, then Sister Jackson called me that the young lady's husband was looking for me. Where is this guy from and where he lives? Sister Jackson said that her husband bought a half million dollars life insurance, but she lived again so he got mad. Since that day, no one can go to his house again. The demonic always finds the way to use husbands or wives to kill one another until all vanished. All homicide and suicide are demon's work.

Sometimes, they can use deacons or pastors who do not believe in the Holy Spirit or miracles to block the Lord's real workers from doing the job for Him. Even today many people still do not believe in miracle. Some religions teach that the miracle only happened 2000 years ago. They said that today medical is their miracle and hope. Thus, I must be careful about praying for people. Demons are seeking to steal, kill, and destroy. They can use any body to destroy our own family. After 3 years had passed the report said that this lady died and was buried. No report of her sickness or illness or the cause of her death. All we knew was she died and was buried. John 10:8-10. However, God is still the same God and the same healer today as 2000 years ago, and He is the same healer forever. God is the same living God forever.

I thought pray for healing is part of our job to serve the Lord, but it turns to be some's enemy. Well, I should not pray for some one who have cancer again.

Many years later my uncle died in hospital, my auntie ask me to pray, I did, went pray for him and live again, this time his son wants to kill me, since then he never calls by my name but the fuck guy. Because he bought $300k life insurance, because he had to continue to pay on premium for 3 more years. Cancer is demonic influence to human to murder each other, to hate, lies, corruption, so on...

Healing the Appendix

In 1994, Mrs. Meuy Fey was rushed to the Emergency Room of Sutter Memorial Hospital. The attending physicians found that she had an appendix and needed a surgery within 30 minutes, or she would die. However, the surgery rooms were full, and she was rushed to another hospital for surgery. So, her parents called me to pray for her. I did pray for her while I was driving to see her. As soon I arrived at the emergency room, others and I prayed for her. While we were praying, she saw a big hand touching her face and felt hot heat from her head all the way down to her stomach. Suddenly, her pain was gone, and she was fine. At that moment, the surgeons came to her and tried to perform a surgery on her, but she told them that her pain was gone. She was fine and no longer needed the surgery. The surgeons were so shocked and examined her and found that her Appendix was gone and no longer there. She was discharged from the hospital without the surgery. This tells us that when we pray with faith and believe that God can do all things, then God does make it possible as the Bible says, "With man this is impossible, but with God all things are possible (Mat 19:26, Mk 11:22, James 5:13-16).

Please see Mey Fey Saechao's letter and picture after her letter below.

Hi Pastor,

I hope this email finds you and family well. Please feel free to edit, my grammars are not so good. Thank you.

Meuy Saechao

My life before my family accepted Christ Jesus, I remember my mom running down the street several times chasing my dad with a bb gun. My mom had a temper problem and dad always knew what to say and do to set her off so my brother, sister and I were mother fearing children.

In May 1994, Pastor Seng helped my family accepted Christ Jesus into our lives; I was 14 years old and knew nothing about Christ Jesus.

My life took a turn when I notice my mother's temper was getting better a few months after accepting Christ Jesus. She was praying more and more, and she was so calm and at peace; that was when I realize maybe there is a God, so I started really seeking Christ Jesus myself. I found myself praying in my heart more and more and overcoming obstacles in school. I also found myself praying for others.

In early 1995, I was diagnosed with appendicitis and the hospital's x-ray confirmed I needed surgery right away. While the nurses were preparing surgery and the surgeon on his way, I was left in a room for only a few minutes before I was being moved to the next room for my surgery... I remember asking in my heart "please God, take this pain away". It was then... just a few seconds later...the lights in my room seemed to dim because there was a much brighter lightheaded towards me. Right before I closed my eyes as my they were too sensitive to the bright light, I realize it was a hand coming towards me and I felt numbness from the top of my head going through my body and exited my toes, the pain disappeared immediately. When the nurses came back in my room to relocate me to surgery, I let them know the pain was gone and I knew that i no longer needed the surgery. They gave me another x-ray and confirmed that there were no traces of appendix issue, they were puzzled and discharged me. I remember stepping out into the waiting room, Pastor Seng and a few others were out in the waiting room praying for me.

"Dear Heavenly Father, I ask for your blessing upon Pastor Seng that he might receive the rest that he needs from his long hours of work, I pray that he is able to eat right and get proper exercise so that he can remain healthy for Your work. Please hold Pastor Seng in the palm of your hands as he continually walks by faith, knowing that you will provide for his every need as well as the needs of his family. I pray through Jesus's name, Amen." Ps. 91:11 / Lk. 10:19

Thank you, Pastor Seng, for everything!
Belove, Meuy Saechao

Cancer Can Move Around and Talk

In 1994, we went to a person who had cancer, and his doctor told him that he had only about 2 months to live. We sang some hymn and made a devotion to the Lord God before praying for him. Suddenly, he declared that his pain moved from his shoulder down to his thigh already. I was wondered why it happened that way because we had not even laid our hands on him and prayed for him yet. We, then laid our hands on his thigh and prayed for him. As soon as we prayed, he declared that his pain moved from the thigh up to the back. We moved our hands up to the back and prayed, then he said that his pain had moved to the leg.

Finally, we stop praying and asked him to confess his sins to the Lord God and he did. He confessed all his sins to the Lord God, then we laid our hands on him and prayed for him again. This time he said that his pain no longer moved around in his body but gone. He no longer had pain. He was healed. Furthermore, he got up and started to prepare a meal and told us to eat with him. We were so happy that he was healed back to normal within only about 10 minutes. We, then learned that his sins were the demons and the demons were the sins as they are one family. The demons made him sick and in pain. The demons also moved his pain around his body to avoid the healing power of God when we prayed for him. That's why he was not healed when we prayed for him at first.

He had to confess all his sins to the Lord God and God commanded the demons to stop moving around and he was completely healed. Then, we went to pray for another lady who was a deaconess and important person for her church, but she was so sick. This time, we did not go ahead and prayed for her but asked her to see whether she had any sins. She answered that she did not have any sins. We, then prayed for her, but her pain was still there and still bothering her.

Furthermore, we heard that her voice was not a female's voice, but a man's voice. That man's voice was more powerful than our voice. So, we prayed for her and encouragement for our team, then asked her about her past. She told us that during her childhood, her parents dedicated her to the spirit with a vow for the spirit to protect her. We, then helped her cancel all her vows and prayed for her. This time, her pain was suddenly gone, and she was healed.

Most of the Asians believe in their ancestral spirits. They also believe that their ancestral spirits protect them, bless them, and heal them. On the other hand, their ancestral spirits are very strict in calling for payments whenever they provided protection, healing and blessing to their family. Most of the families don't know the amount of compensation they need to pay their ancestral spirits, and the spirits let the demons make them sick and ill with cancer and other diseases. Demons do not have cousins, and they are the two-edge sword of ancestral spirits that kill all the peoples in the world. They don't care if we are white, black, Asian, poor or rich, clever or dumb, educated or ordinary persons as long someone has anger, madness, resentment, and other sins as the highway for cancers to travel into life. The only way to protect people from spirits, demons, and diseases is the prayer and faith in the Lord Jesus all the time. We also need to always stay away from the troublemakers and their violence.

Fighting with Demons All Night Long

One morning in 1995, two ladies knocked on the door and my wife opened it for them to come into our home. One of the ladies told us that she had cancer in her stomach and asked us for her healing prayers. She also told us that she learned from others that I had always prayed for other people and their cancer healings. She supposed to go to her own church for prayers but did not because no one was helpful. She decided to go to me at my home for a private prayer because she didn't want to expose her privacy to others as she might have to face a shame. So, I put my hands on her stomach where the pain was, then prayed for her. At the middle of my prayer, I felt that something went out from my hand to her, suddenly, her pain was gone within 5 minutes, and she was healed, then went home.

However, that night I couldn't sleep. I was half asleep and half awaken because I felt like a small boy came and fought with me like a little monkey all night long. The naked small boy was very powerful and always overcame me. In fact, he was a demon which played around with me in the house. When I slept, he slept. When I sat, he sat. When I stood, he stood. When I stopped, he stopped, too. I did not want to fight with him and prayed all night long, but it did not work until about 3 AM in the morning, then I realized that the only way to get him off me was a loud command prayer. I, then prayed with a loud commanded,

"In the NAME OF JESUS CHRIST WHO DIED ON THE CROSS BY HIS BLOOD YOU DEMONS GET OUT OF HERE NOW, NOW, NOW, NOW, and now! I command you in the name of JESUS."

At that moment, I saw that he jumped out of the window, disappeared, and gone. About a year later, the lady told me that her cancer was healed at moment after my prayer. She was healthy and still working around the yard and go to church every Sunday. I, then learned that cancers are the demons that go around the global to find places to stay and they stay in the bodies of the people who have sins, but do not have strong faith in Jesus Christ the Lord as the Bible states that the thief comes only to steal, kill, and destroy; I have come that they may have life, and have to the full (John 10:8-10 NIV).

Special Forgiveness for My Bad Neighbor

In 1995, there was a bad neighbor who lived next to my home and close to a park. He committed burglary, stealing, and fighting all the time. He broke into my garage and stole my car stereo, tools, my son's bike and so on. My family saw him with their eyes, but he refused to return the items to us. I thought that I bought my house there by mistake and wanted to sell it, but no one bought it. I, then prayed to God for help and God answered my prayers. One day, someone gave me 2 bags of shrimps. We ate a bag, and I took the other bag to the bad neighbor. He accepted it from me and asked, "Are you giving it to me?" I said, "Yes." He asked, "How much?" I said, "Free." He, then said, "Thank you, thank you, and thank you." He seemed quite shocked about my hospitality toward him.

After that day, he no longer stole any more things from me and my family. Nothing was missing from our home and yard again. Furthermore, that bad neighbor became my good friend and guard. He even watched our home and belongings for us while we were gone. Sometimes, he even chased the people who parked in front of my home without my permission away so my friends who visited me could park there. At first, I thought that I bought that house there by mistake and hated it, but after that bad neighbor became my friend and helped me, then I loved it and lived there for a long time until I sold it not very long ago. This lesson leads me to realize that God and God's words are so good for me and the world, "But I tell you, love your enemies and pray for those who persecute you, that you may be children of your Father in heaven." (**Mat 5:43-47**).

Left My Full-Time Job

In 1995, while I was working as a drug counselor, a voice came to me, "Quit your job and serve me." I knew immediately that, that voice was from the Lord God. I asked, "If you are the Lord God and you want me to leave my Job and serve you, please give me a confirmation through a man." I, then asked one of the elders of my church and he said, "Yes, I want you to leave your job and serve God full time." However, I still was not sure and waited for another confirmation, I thought of Samuel who anointed David as king, but God did not let him be the king until about a decade later.

While, I was waiting for another confirmation, I went to downtown Sacramento with a deacon of my church. While we were on the way, the deacon said to me, Pastor, our church discussed about a pastor for our church. We want you to be our pastor. We want you to quit your job and serve God full time. Our church will pay you the same salary as your current job. I knew that this call was from God, then I gave my notice to my boss and my boss conveyed it to the whole work group. Everybody at work was so shock and my boss asked me, "Why do you quit the job? Is there anything wrong at work? Is this your personal decision?" "No." I answered. "I am being called by the Lord God to quit my job and serve Him full time." Then I left the job and have been serving the Lord as His call for 20 years now.

I have been studying the Bible, fasting, and praying for the sick and needy. I taught the Bible to our church, including the head of the deacons who told me to quit my job that God would provide. Later his friends and he left our church, and our church was half empty after their departure. After that, our church could no longer pay my full salary to me as their promise. So, they bought rice and other foods for me, instead. Once, I was out of money and foods to eat. I held on to an empty rice bag and prayed, "My Lord God, do you see? My rice bag is empty, no more rice in it. Will you, please send me some rice?" Two hours after my prayer, I found a whole bag of rice sitting in front of my entrance door. I picked it up, took it inside, and prayed, "My Lord God, the rice is here, but no other foods. How about the beef, pork and other foods?" The next day my church members took a lot of beef, pork and other foods to me at my home.

However, I continued to fast and prayed to God, "What is my wrongdoing? What is the price I must pay?" But there were no answers to my prayer. I, then confessed my sins to the Lord with tears for years. Once, I fasted and prayed for 25 days, then I heard a gentle voice from the Lord that I needed to go to the church and wash my mother's feet. I hurriedly went to the church and worship the Lord with my congregation in the afternoon. I told my wife, and she brought me a bowl of water. I washed my mother's feet and saw my mother's light shone like the angels of the Lord. At that moment, I felt like I was touched by the Lord right there. When I touched my mother's feet, I was shocked by the electric from the head through my whole body. I washed my sister's feet, then father-in-law's feet, elders and deacons, and the whole church. At that moment, I felt I was a man of a total sin, not even a spot was clean. I felt like my whole body was dead. I confessed my sins again with sobbing and tears. I continued my fasting and praying up to 40 days and then, I felt like I was in a total peace and joy with the Lord in heaven.

Well, two months after my washing of feet for my mother and the whole church, my mother died in peace on December 25, 2003. God has been helping and blessing my church from the time our church was half emptied to today. God has filled our church with more and more faithful members than those who left long time ago. God has been so faithful and good to me and my church. God has been answering my prayers every time and right away. He is the living God forever.

Miraculous Reunion with My Wife

One day in 1998, my wife and I had a small argument that led to a quarrel and madness, finally. She was unable to control her temper and neither me. We had some other minor arguments before, but none of them was as major as this one. We could not reconcile and prayed both separately and as a couple, but no solution and reconciliation. We, then called our church elders for counseling, but it did not help, either. Her parents counseled us, too, but it did not make any difference. Our whole church prayed for us, but we just could not agree on anything. We went to Thailand and sought prayers from the special anointed pastors, but our arguments got worst, and we no longer wanted to see each other. We hated each other so much that we decided to get divorce.

We agreed that after the divorce, both of our sons would live with me and our only daughter would live with her. She, then bought an airplane ticket for flying away from me to another state so she would not have to see me again. I thought the same until it was almost midnight that night, I started feeling a remorse about my offensive behavior toward her. I, then tried my best to find a special word to say to her so she will remember me in time of good and bad after our divorce. Finally, I decided to just say, **"I love you"** to her. I, then looked at her, but she did not look at me. She even turned her back on me because she was so mad at me. However, I said **"Honey, I love you"** and at that very moment a soft and gentle voice came from somewhere like an old man's voice, "Say it again!" The voice was so strange because I had never heard it before in my life. I looked around and through the whole room without seeing any one in site.

However, I thought to myself that it would not hurt to say what I had just said to her again. I, then said, **"Honey, I love you."** This time,

I felt something happened inside my stomach like a burst of water spring that flooded my stomach up to my chest and about to flow out of my mouth. The water was sweeter than the honey. I, then forgot the problems with my wife and focused on the sweet honey in my mouth that I could not explain at that time and even now. I was wondered what it was so special like that. I, then said to her for the third times, **"I love you,"** then my heart was full of the Holy Ghost, love compassion, and forgiveness. I looked at my wife and saw that she was so young and beautiful, but so lonely and so desperately needed me and my help. I, then cried with a loud voice to her that I was so sorry for all those wrong things that said and did to her and our families. Then, I said, **"Honey, I really love you.** I have just realized that I have been wrong on everything. Please forgive me and all the wrong things that I said and did to you." We, then embraced each other and cried for a night long and reconciled. In the morning, we told our children everything, then asked them for forgiveness, too. They were so kind and forgave us without any problems. I went outside and saw that the trees and flowers were full of beauty of God. I saw everything changed in color and all things became new creation of God, full of joy and happiness that I had never had before. The miracle of God, "With man this is impossible, but with God all things are possible." (**Mat 19:26**)

Healing a Man With Stroke

Foucho Saechao healed from a stroke in 1997.

In 1997, my neighbor cousin called me that one of our neighbors got stroke and was rushed to the Methodist hospital. All of his family members followed him to hospital and learned from the attending physicians that he had a major stroke, and his brain was full of blood. He might not even make it through that night. There was no hope for his survival. No surgeries would be needed. So, his family asked me to pray for him, and I did. I went to the hospital and prayed for him overnight together with family and elders, then a few times a day for a week. The doctor told me that the patient was almost dead, and it made no sense for me to keep on praying for days like that, but we did not stop. We continued our prayers for him and so the family. Ten days later the doctor was so mad about the prayer, but the patient regained his consciousness. He was discharged from the hospital and went home only 14 days later. He returned to his doctor for a follow up appointment; his doctor told him that his stroke was clear. The stroke was no longer shown on his X-ray. He had his stroke on January 6, 1997, but has been still living until today. Now, we know that the doctor could not do anything about the stroke, but the Living God can because He is the Holy God. No one in heaven and on the earth have such a healing power as Jesus Christ the Savior. All things are possible for Him. He has the power over everything, even the stroke and the dead is able to rise again.

Letter from Foucho's Daughter

My father Fou cho Saechao had a stroke on January 6, 1997, at 55 years old. My family did not know the severity of the stroke until we arrived at the hospital. After hours in the waiting room the doctor brought us the news. The blood had filled my father's brain and that there was nothing the doctors could do to save him and for my family members to go see him because he might not make it through the night. We know that God heals and performs miracles, so my mom called our Pastor and the elders of the church to pray and agree for a miracle.

We felt the anointing of God as we prayed and cried out to him during that hour in the ER room. Through the grace of God, he lived through the night; however, he was in a coma for two weeks. During this time church members gathered at our house nightly to pray, singing songs of worship unto the Lord, believing and expecting a miracle. I remember praying in tongues to God and stood on the scripture Luke 1:37 "with God nothing is impossible". One day while visiting my father with the pastor and elders, his doctor asked us if anything should happen to my father and he stops breathing that we give them permission to not perform CPR on him. Their prognosis is that if he lives, he will be in a vegetation status and not be able to do anything on his own and will require assistance to live. With faith inside my heart and eyes focused on Jesus's healing power, I answered the doctor, "we have prayed and it's all in Jesus's hands". His situation in the natural aspect did not look or sound good, but in the spiritual realm God was working in him.

Hallelujah glory to Jesus, my dad was out of a coma in two weeks and breathing on his own. My father came home with a feeding tube but was not able to talk or walk yet. As we continue to pray and worship God, in a short period of time he was able to eat, walk and talk. We witnessed God's love and the healing power in my father's life. After a month later he went back to the hospital to do a CT scan to his brain and the test results showed that the blood had cleared up and everything is normal. Jesus supernaturally performed surgery on him. My dad is a living proof that there is nothing impossible with God. The doctor's had given up on him but 17 years later at the age of 72 he is alive and well, God's word is so true. All we must do is ask and believe and God will deliver.

We are so blessed and grateful to have the support of our Pastor and church members that gathered with us nightly to praise, worship and agree that Jesus will perform a miracle for my dad. We give all the glory and all the praise to our Lord and savior Jesus Christ.

From Foucho's family

Changing Flight to Sacramento

In 1998, I was called by God to go on a mission trip to Thailand. My wife wanted to go with me, but we did not have enough money to buy her round-trip airplane ticket. We exhausted our efforts but did not let any other people know about it. I prayed to God for the needed money, "My Lord God, my wife wants to go to Thailand and serve you with me, but we don't have enough money to buy her round-trip airplane ticket. In the name of Jesus Christ, please provide a gift of $1,000.00 to us so we can buy her ticket, Amen." The next day, I took an elderly couple of our church to a store, then to the doctor. Between the way, the couple gave an envelope to me. I asked, "What is this for?" They replied, "It's for your trip to Thailand. Last night, at about 10:30PM God told us to give this $1,000.00 to you for your trip. That's why we are giving it to you now." I told them that it's too much. I wanted to accept only $800.00, but they insisted that I accepted all $1,000 as the way God told them. I, then accepted the money and tried to buy the round-trip airplane ticket for flying from Sacramento, California to Thailand; but it was more expensive. So, we bought the tickets for flying from San Jose, California to Thailand.

After our mission in Thailand and while we were waiting to get on the airplane at Bangkok, Thailand, I told all the 15 others in my group that I felt that it was a burden for our children to have to drive two hours to San Jose, California and pick us up to go home in Sacramento. I did not want to go to San Jose, but I will go to Sacramento, Ca. I, then prayed, "My Lord God, we have just finished fulfilling your mission and ready to fly back to the USA, but I don't want to burden my children and don't want to go through San Jose. In the name of Jesus Christ, may we fly directly back to Sacramento, Ca, please? Amen." After my prayer, 14 others in my group said, "We don't believe that the airline of your airplane ticket will let you fly back to Sacramento, Ca. If God let you do so, we will buy you a pig and give you a big feast after we get home." I warned them that in the name of Jesus Christ, please prepare to buy the pig and hold the feast for me soon. We, then got on the airplane from Bangkok to Tokyo. When we got to Tokyo, the airline staff told us that the flight to San Jose was cancelled. We had to fly from Tokyo to Seattle, WA, then put us on the airplane to Sacramento as my prayer. When we got to Sacramento, I asked everyone about my pig, but they all smiled and left for their homes without giving it to me until today. The Bible says, "The heart is deceitful above all things and beyond cure. Who can understand it?" (Jeremiah 17:9), but God is faithful "I AM WHO I AM." (Ex 3: 14).

Healing a Hmong Boy

One day in 1999, a Hmong boy had a cramp on both of his legs while he was playing in the field of a school. The pain got better, and he went home. When he arrived home, his pain became worse and worse, and finally, he became unconscious and was rushed in an ambulance to an Emergency Room of a hospital for treatment. The attending Physicians could not find the cause and could not revive him. They thought that he had a blood clot in the vein of his legs and performed a surgery on both legs. They still could not find anything wrong in the legs and performed a surgery on both of his hands, too. A month later, he was still in coma. Furthermore, he lost almost all of his weight and was so skinny that his eyes popped out, too. It was so scary. The doctors told his family that his brain was dead, and they could no longer do anything for him. They suggested that his family let them unplug all of his life support and let him die in peace. His family loved him so much and did not want to do so and called for a decision-making meeting among the whole family members, cousins, schoolteachers, doctors, nurses, child protective services, priests, and welfare workers to discuss about the life of the boy.

Almost all of the 20 people in the meeting agreed that they had no more hope for the boy's survival and needed to prepare for his funeral service from that day. Only his parents who loved him so much and refused to let the doctors unplug the life support. They requested that the doctors cut off the boy's legs and arms and see if it would help him regain his consciousness and live. At first, I thought to myself that even such major surgeries on the boy, still couldn't save his life, what else can be done. I, then asked to see whether any better doctors in northern California or the whole U.S might be able to help, but those attending physicians and surgeons said that even the best doctors from the University hospital of San Francisco had been there already but could not do anything. At this point, my mind kept on wondering what kind of disease it was that had caused such awful illness. Finally, **I asked all the people at the meeting for permission to ask my boss to help the boy.** The doctors asked me, **"Who is your boss?"** I answered, **"Jesus Christ of Nazareth is my boss."**

The doctors all laughed at me and said that it was so funny to say so because they did not believe that He could help. However, they told me to go ahead and call my boss to help the boy. To them, it was funny, but to us it was a true faith in the Lord, Mark 11:22 "Have faith in God," Jesus answered. 23 "Truly I tell you, if anyone says to this mountain, 'Go, throw yourself into the sea,' and does not doubt in their heart but believes that what they say will happen, it will be done for them. 24 Therefore I tell you, whatever you ask for in prayer, believe that you have received it, and it will be yours." (Mk 11:22-24) and 26 Jesus looked at them and said, "With man this is impossible, but with God all things are possible." (Mat 19:26). For example, when the giant Goliath saw that a little boy David was there to fight him, he thought that it was so funny to him, but the little boy David won over him. David cut off his head and King Saul's army won the war over the Philistines (1 Sam 17:46-47). So, I went inside the room and put my hand on the boy's stomach, then prayed for him, but I felt that there was a person who was on top of the boy. I opened my eyes and looked, but there was no one there except the boy alone. I, then put my hand on top of the boy and prayed again and still felt that the person was still there on top of the boy again to block me from reaching the boy.

However, I did not give up. I put my hand on the boy, closed my eyes, and prayed for him for the third time. This time, I did not open my eyes and kept on praying, thanking and calling Jesus the

Lord God to please answer my prayer and heal the boy. About ten minutes after my prayer, others and I walked out of the room and went home. About 2 weeks later, I heard good news from the boy's parents that the boy had regained consciousness, opened his eyes, and understood about what was going on around him already. The boy was discharged from the hospital and went home about 2 months after my prayer. His family celebrated his recovery with a big feast. The boy and his family were all rejoiced and happy together. The boy was able to go back to school and played sports again. The living God is Jesus Christ who died on the cross for you and me. Praise the lord God who is living today and forever Amen (Mat 8:17).

Miracle Fish

IIn 1999, after I left my full-time job and accepted a full-time job with my church, my church split into two groups. My church membership was about half less and no longer be able to pay me my full-time salary. I no longer had enough money to afford my living; I just lived by faith. One day, I went to a store and tried to buy some things that I needed. I saw some fish and I wanted to buy the fish, too. The 4 pounds fish was $15.00, but I had only $5.00 now. I had been eating this kind of fish for about 20 years in Laos and Thailand. I loved eating it, but did not have enough cash to buy it. I thought of borrowing some money from someone that I knew but could not find one inside the store. I asked the store clerk to cut the fish in haft so I could buy it, but he refused to do so. I, then walked out to the outside of the store to find someone, but could not find anyone, either. I walked into the store again to look but still could not find any.

I, then went home with a sadness and disappointment. That night, I could not sleep because my mind kept on thinking about the delicious fish. Early in the next morning, my phone rang. I picked it up and answered it. The caller was my cousin. He said, "Do you want to eat fish?" I answered, "Yes. What kind of fish?" He said, "Just bring some big garbage bags in your Toyota Pick Up Truck to me and I will give you some fish." I said, "Ok, I will come right now." I, then was wondered why he told me to bring my Toyota Pick Up Truck and big garbage bags. However, I did as the way he told me and went to him. When I got to my cousin's home, he gave me a lot of fish that I wanted to eat. Each of them was 10 times bigger than the one I saw at the store.

I asked him, "Where do you get these fish from?" He said, "Somebody got a boatful of them from the Bay Area, but he does not have any place to put them. He dumped them in my house. I asked, "How much each?" He said, "Free. No charge. Go ahead and take as many as you want." I took about 30. Each of them was about 20 pounds or more. I could carry only one each time. I invited about 50 relatives and friends to have a dinner with me that day. I also gave each of them some fish to take home, too. After that but I still had a lot left for myself. This is God's miracle through Jesus Christ that Jesus fed five thousand people with two small fish and a few loaves of bread and there were still twelve basketfuls of foods left (Mat 13-21 Mk 6:30-44 Lk 9:10-17 John 6:1-15).

In covid 19 time, I just stay home, so I plan to go for fishing for striped bass. I learn how to fish myself. I fish at a spot but never caught one, but one guy fish at a place about 30 feet from me. He caught one then caught other one. I think in my mind lord just give his 2 fish then I will go home. I did not talk, I just think in head. Suddenly, that guy brought his 2 fish to me. He said uncle I only fish for fun, you can take home. Only limited 2 per day. And 18 inches and up.

One week later I went the same spot but different guy fishing in there. He continues get 1 and 2 second one but I didn't get any. I think in my head if that guy gives his fish to me then I will go home. Suddenly, he brought 2 fish to me, he said, uncle you can have it. I want to continue to fish. if not, I can't stay my limited is over. So, I took the fish then go home.

A week later. I didn't go same spot any more but different place, everywhere people pack. It was busy. I think in my head Lord help me to find a good spot, keep think. I look there was a guy prepare to go home. I ask, are you going home? He said yes, I ask how your fishing go? He said no not luck. While he packs to go. I hurry prepare my fishing pole and bait. I just throw fishing line about 30 feet then I caught one 22 inches. Then second one about 20 inches. The law allows 18 inches up. While the guy still there. He asks is that the way you fish?. He said, I fish since this morning but get nothing, and I lost all my weight. He said seems joke to me, he said I can't believe it. when God lead all things are easy and all things are possible. God always help in time of need not time of wanted. So may time, we people want more never enough. I have prayed or think something, I just want it more, but God not give it to me.

Destroyed the Cross in 1999
First Case

A church member called me that his whole family could not sleep for a few nights already because they heard that a lot of demons were in their home. They called a few deacons of their church to pray for them at their home, but it did not help. The demons were still in their home and bothered them. They, then called me to pray for them. As soon as my prayer team and I arrived at their home, we felt a chill in our bodies and our hair were flying. We used the olive oil to anoint the whole home and prayed, then we went home. The family was calm for a few days, then they heard the demons again and could not sleep again. They called me to pray for them again.

This time, I told all the deacons to wait for me outside of that home until I arrived and they did. After my arrival to that home, we anointed everybody before we went into the home. As I was walking along the hallway inside, I felt a chill again. I felt that my head became bigger one moment and smaller at another moment, and my hair flying again, too. Even I was with others in that home, but I felt like I was alone at a cemetery at the middle of the night. I asked all of the people inside that home to see whether they had the same feeling as me and they all said that they did have the same feeling as me, too. We, then sang a few hymns and prayed without the weird feeling gone. I asked all the people in that home to see if they had any objects that they used for the spirit worship in the past or not. A little boy answered that he saw a cross on top of some flowers that looked like funeral flowers and brought it home. The boy gave that cross to me and we burned it, then prayed for his whole family, then we went home. That night his whole family slept peacefully without hearing the demons again. They have been in peace ever since.

Second Case

Once, I visited my sister-in-law in Seattle, Washington and I saw that she was walking with a pair of clutches. I asked her, "What is wrong with you?" She replied, "I could not walk and went to the hospital, but the doctors could not find anything wrong and could not help me. I still must walk with this pair of clutches." My prayer group of about 10 people sang a few hymns and prayed for her, then she stood up and walked without the clutches in her apartment. Furthermore, she walked with us to another brother-in-law's home without using the clutches and any problems. She was healed and was very happy.

Later she went out and returned home. Upon her arrival at home, she felt a heavy thing came on her shoulders, she fell to the ground, could not get up and could not walk again from that moment on. My brother in-law called me to pray for her again. We went to her home and asked her that there must be something in her home that belonged to the demons. She said that she had three crosses in her home because she thought that as a Christian, she should have them at her home, and she put them in her living room. I told her that I was not against the cross, but if she believed that Jesus was in those three crosses and believed in those crosses more than Jesus and God, then her belief was wrong, and it was against Jesus and God. She should not keep those crosses in her home but throw them away. We, then destroyed them with a hammer and burned them, then prayed for her. After that she started walking and has been walking until today. Thus, we know that the Cross itself has no meaning, but if we believe it more than our Lord Jesus and God, then it becomes problems (Exo 20:5, Levit 19:4 & 26:1). Also, cross made by my brother. Its need to purify by priest or never burn incense. anything burn incense, its will against holy spirit

My House's Mortgage Paid Off Through a Miracle

In 2001, the same house that I lived in for so long, I was so tired of living in it. So, I prayed to the Lord God for help to sell it, "My Lord God, I would like a $30,000 loan from you so I may pay-off the loan of my current house and buy another one somewhere that I want to live." Two days after my simple, but truthful prayer, a lady came knock on the door of my home. I opened the door and welcome her in, then asked her to see what she might need from me. She answered that she had some money, but did not have any safe place to keep them. She would like me to help her keep them until she needed them. I asked her, "If I kept them for you, may I use them for pay off the house?" She replied, "Yes, you may use it as the way you see appropriate until I need it, may be ten years from now."

So, I counted the money and found that it was exactly $30,000.00 dollars in cash. I accepted the money then pay off the house and sold it and look for a new house. I found a new bigger house that cost more than what I had from that lady and my other savings. I loved to buy that new big house but had no way to afford it. I, then prayed to God for help with a confidence, "My Lord God, please give me a $10,000.00 gift in cash so I can buy the new bigger house that I want. Please give me a gift, not a loan because I cannot afford any more loans." After my prayer, I signed the contract of buying the new bigger house in cash and set an appointment for paying it off. However, I could not find the needed $10,000.00 dollars from any one and anywhere. I just kept on praying for it every day and night.

As the appointment was approaching, the seller called me for the money, but I told him that I had not had it yet. I will pay it on the closing day. The seller was very upset and called me every day, but each time I told him the same answer. One day, I felt that I needed to go into the house and pray. I, then asked the seller for the key to do so. The seller said, "You are crazy. You have not paid the house in full and ask me for the key already. You must wait until you paid off before getting the key." I kept on my prayers and felt much stronger that I needed to go and clean the house before moving in after the closing date. I asked the seller for the key again to clean the house. He understood well and gave the key to me. My wife and I took the key to the house and started the cleaning from the first floor, then second floor, and finally the third floor. While my wife was cleaning the bathroom on the third floor, she called me, "Dad! I found some money here." I asked, "How much?" She answered, "I don't know yet. It's a lot." So, we counted them and found that they were exactly $10,000.00 that we needed. So, we took the money to the escrow and paid off the house. I even told the seller and the broker about the money that the money was provided by the Lord Jesus Christ after my consistent prayer. They told me that this house was on the market 4 times more than the price that I bought, but no one bought it. They also believed that God wanted my wife and to have the house. Thus, we know and believe that our living Lord Jesus Christ is the true Son of God and God who made heaven and earth and Universe.

Miracle Lunch With My Wife

One day in 2001, my wife and I went and prayed for our church members from morning to about noon, then returned home. When we got home, we were exhausted and hungry, but no foods yet. I pointed my finger to the telephone and prayed, "Whoever has a lunch ready, please call me now, in the name of Jesus Christ, Amen." Suddenly, the phone rang. I answered it and heard the caller said, "Have you eaten your lunch yet?" I answered, "No, not yet. We have just returned from the church." He said, "We have been looking for you all morning, but could not find you until now. It's good that you have just returned home. Please come and eat with me. Please come now." We, then went to the caller's home and found that he had a buffet, full of different kind of foods such hot-pot with spicy shrimps, fish, meat, onion, vegetables, and so on. We thanked the Lord then ate. Those foods were so delicious, and we were so full. This is what the Bible says, "Give, and it will be given to you. A good measure, pressed down, shaken together and running over, will be poured into your lap. For with the measure you use, it will be measured to you." When we give to God, God gives back ten folds (Luk 6:38; Deu 28:1-14).

Healing Cancer

In 2004, a man name Fu Hiang Saechao called the head deacon of our church that he wanted to accept the Lord Jesus Christ as his savior, then his cancer healing prayer. He said that he had cancer and went to many other religious people for prayers for about two years without being healed. His cancer got worse and worse. Since his doctor told him that he had only about six months to live, he wanted to try Jesus Christ and see whether the Christ would heal him. When we got together in the house, he accepted Jesus Christ through a regular worship and burning of his spiritual materials, including antiques. He was healed right after his acceptance of Jesus Christ and prayer. He was jumping and dancing with happiness. He also cooked foods and ate with us, then went home. He was fine for 7 days, then got sick again. He called me to help him. My prayer team and I went to his home and prayed for him. This time, we asked him whether he had any more antiques or ever cursed someone. He said yes, he did curse his brother-in-law who cheated him $10,000.00 dollars and another businessman who cheated him $15,000.00 dollars. He cursed them that their stomach be broken due to their cheatings of him.

The businessman's stomach did break while he was in a hospital, but his brother-in-law's stomach had not been broken, but in some severe pain and was almost dead. We explained to him that a curse is like a two-edge sword that curses both sides. Since he cursed two people, those two curses were cutting him, too, with a cancer. He needed to pray and confess his sins before Jesus would heal him. He complied fully and Jesus healed him from his cancer. Five days later, he called again, and we went to his home again. This time, we asked him about his antique and he apologized that he still had some Buddha idols on the walls and some other antiques in his possession, too. So, we helped him burn all of those Buddha idols and antiques, then prayed for him and he was healed again.

This time, he was doing very well for about 2 ½ years, then he forgot about Jesus Christ and the Bible. He went to a casino, gamble, and won a lot of money, but came home with a lot of pain in his body. He went back to his doctor and asked for pain pills. The doctor gave him 4 pain pads and told him to just put one pad on him a day, but he put all 4 pads on his body at once. A few days after that, he was so sick and went back to doctor. The doctor examined him and told him that his internal organs were cooking like a cooking pot due to his putting of all those 4 pain pads on him at once, not four times as the doctor's recommendation. The doctor could not help him again and he died during that week. This leads us to know that the evil spirits are always looking for ways to steal, kill, and destroy (John 10:8-10).

Another man had the same cancer and sickness. He asked for healing prayer and our prayer team prayed for him. He abided by all the instructions in the Bible and from us. He did not hide anything. He let us burn all of his spiritual materials, including antiques away, then he was healed completely. He has been doing so well and has been healthy for over 10 years now.

Welcome Jesus to Lunch

In 2004, I thought of what the Lord God had helped me so many things and so many times in my life. I, then thought that I would like to welcome Jesus Christ to a lunch and give a special thanks to him in person. I prayed to the Lord Jesus, "My Lord, tomorrow at noon, I would like to welcome you to have a lunch with me. Lord don't be late because the food may get cold. I would like to thank you with a special thanks."

The next day, I prepared 3 choices of foods for serving the Lord Jesus Christ. I also prepared everything in pairs such as a pair of plates, a pair of chairs, a pair of folks, and a pair of chopsticks for the Lord and me. When the foods were ready, I put everything on the table, then prayed "My Lord, the lunch is ready. I am specially thanking You for everything that You have helped and done for me. You are the answer. Now, I would like to give you my special thanks one on one. I have owed you so much but have nothing to give back to you. I only have this lunch to thank you with. Please go ahead and eat with me." After my prayer, I saw that nothing happened.

I, then prayed again for the second time, nothing happens, either. I kept on praying for the third time, "My Lord, you are from the Middle East, but I am from Asia. The foods I have prepared for You are not from Asia and neither Middle east, but from the bottom of my heart. They are a little spicy, but please try them." At that moment, I heard someone knocked on my entrance door. I hurriedly went and opened it up and saw a lady standing at the door. The lady said, "May I come in?" I replied, "Sure, please come in." She came in and said, "I come to see your wife. Where is your wife?" I replied, "My wife is not home."

She, then asked, "Why do you set everything up in pairs on the table." I answered, "One is for you!" She said, "Someone invited me to have lunch with them at another place, but I come here to talk to your wife for a business before I go there. Since you have a lunch ready, I will enjoy it with you before I go there." We, then had lunch together. After the lunch, she said that the foods were a little too spicy, but other than that everything was fine. She, then left. Since that day, every time I pray, God answered me, God answers all of my prayers. He answers even the small things I ask such as bamboo shoot, lemon, noodle and so on.

Demons In the Silver Bars and Gold Coins

In 2004, one of the older ladies in my church was active, helpful, and honorable. She donated $1,000. to my airfare when I went on a mission trip. One day she called me, "I need your prayer because the doctor reported that I have to get dialysis." Since I was driving in the freeway, I couldn't talk in detail but hurriedly explained to her that as soon as she called me, I had a feeling in my heart that she still had some spiritual items in her possession. Please go ahead and look around her home for the demonic belongings while she was waiting for me. She got mad and said, "I burned all my spiritual items away when I accepted Jesus Christ 25 years ago."

"How can you say that I keep some demonic items in my home?" She, then hung up the phone without agreeing to look for anything. A week later, she called me again, "Pastor, you told me last week that I might still had some demonic or spiritual items in my home. I did not believe you, but I thought very hard and remember that after I bought my two silver bars, then my health began to change. I have been sick more and more often, getting worse and worse. Now, it has come to the worst and my appetite is so bad. I have lost so much weight, become frail and so weak. Furthermore, I need to get dialysis three times a week."

So, my two friends and I went to her home and asked, "Where are the silver bars? Please give them to me." She showed them to me, and I saw that they were very old and dark because she just kept them in her possession without cleaning them. At that moment, my friends felt some things quite weird. We burned the silver bars and prayed for her, then she was healed. She went to her doctor, but her doctor could no longer find anything wrong with her blood. The doctor asked, "What did you do? Your blood is normal now. You don't have go to dialysis, just go home. You are fine now, my lady." She went home without dialysis and was healthy again. We explained to her that since her silver bars were sacrificed to the demons and spirits before, they are offensive to God because God does not like anything that offered to other gods. We suggested that she throw them away into the garbage cans, but she refused to do so. She gave them to her cousins who were not Christians. Her cousins offered the silver bars to their spirits again. Many months later, she went to her cousin's home for a thanksgiving feast, then she became ill and went to see her doctor who declared to her that she had to go and get dialysis. She confessed her sins to God, but did not get any answer from God again. She, then had to get dialysis three times a week until she passed away. I did pray for forgiveness from God for her, but God did not answer again. She passed away without getting the forgiveness from God. She was trapped by the demons until her death.

Now, we know that the old lady's case was just like King Saul's case. King Saul had called on the mediums to help him which made God so mad at him and dethroned him. Thus, we need to avoid buying or accepting old silver bars, old gold bars, jewelries, and other antiques that might be offered to spirits and demons to avoid offending God which can bring curse onto us.

Healing My Food Poison

One day in 2004, I ordered and ate a chicken sandwich for lunch at a McDonald Restaurant, then I felt nausea, drowsy, vomited and could not open my eyes. I prayed to God many times without being healed. I did pray and commanded the food to get out of my stomach, and I continued vomiting without healing. Finally, I called the church elders to pray for me with singing, then I felt like something like a cotton rope dropped from the heaven into my mouth, twisted around and around slowly down to the bottom of my stomach, then slowly out of my mouth. Then, I was healed and no longer felt nausea and drowsy. This tells us that our church members need one another. We need to ask the people with faith to pray for us when we are sick and ill (James 5:13-16).

Leading an Old friend to Accept Jesus Christ

One of my old friends used to be able to use the black magic and power of the evil spirits to cause fighting between husband and wife even they love each other deeply. In 2005, he called me that he had a bad dream, then became ill and was about to die. He asked me to interpret his bad dream for him without telling me about the dream. I explained to him that God made heaven and earth and everything, including human beings. The first woman and man did not obey God. They listened to a serpent and ate a fruit which brought sin into themselves and their descendants until today. The sin conquered them and their descendants from the beginning until today. The demons came into the world and took control over all human beings and make them dream bad dreams, get sick and die. All human beings need to accept the only Son of God, Jesus Christ to be their Lord and pray to God for forgiveness of their sins before they can be healed.

There is only one God with many names such as God Elohim, God Jehovah, then God the Holy Spirit that gave power to Mary who gave birth to Jesus Christ who is Jehovah Lord, the Salvation. Jesus lived on earth for 33 years, then was crucified and died on the cross for all the sins of human beings, including him, my old friend. Jesus took all the sins of all the human beings away and has set them free, including you and me, then Jesus ascended to heaven to sit on the right side of God. Now Jesus is the King of kings, the Lord of lords, and today Jesus is come as the Holy Spirit (Mat 1:18, John 14:23).

Those who believe and receive God the Son Jesus Christ into their hearts, then the demons will go away from them. I told my old friends that the demons made him ill with a big stomach. For him to get well, he needed to burn all of the things that he used for worshipping spirits and putting the curse on people and accept Jesus Christ into his heart to be his Lord, then the healing would take place. After I told him about God, Jesus Christ, and the Holy Spirit that can take away his sins and heal him, he understood well and said, "I want to accept the Lord Jesus Christ now." I, then helped him burned about a pickup truck load of his little gods, objects, and other materials that he used for worshipping spirits away, then led him into Jesus Christ. I also baptized him in the name of Jesus Christ and the Holy Spirit, then the Holy Spirit did come upon him at that very moment. He yelled, "O, my stomach is shrinking! I am being healed!"

Indeed, his huge stomach which was as huge as a fully pregnant woman's stomach was shrinking. It shrank down to a normal sized and he was healed. After that, I went to my sister's home and stayed overnight there. The next day, my old friend called me again that he was sick again. I told him that I believed that he still had some demonic belongings in his home such as idols that he used for worshipping the demons and spirits. He searched and found three more bags of Buddha, idols, toys and other objects that he brought from China and other parts of Asia. He gave all of them to me and I burned them in fire, then prayed for him and he was healed.

A few days later, he called me again for the third time that he was sick again. This time I prayed to the Lord God that my old friend accumulated so many materials, objects, idols, and Buddha for worshipping the demons for such a long time, he might still had some of those items left in his home that he might not remember where they were, please reveal them to me so I can tell him to get them and burn them in the fire. God, then revealed to me and I saw in my vision that my old friend made a little house in the branch of a tree and put some idols there that he forgot. He took me to the tree and while we were approaching the tree, some voice yelled from the tree, "Pastor Paul Seng Chao is coming to burn our house now! We need to run! Let's run!" I, then saw some of them ran down the hill side, throwing away their cookware, sinks, and other kitchen items down the hill, then ran away.

When I woke up, I went to his home and told him accordingly. He led me to the tree, and we found a little house on the branch of tree. The little house was almost covered up by the skin of the tree. I had to cut the skin of the tree up and found 4 golden Buddha inside the little house. I took the Buddha and incense from behind the tree to pile up together, burned them in fire, then I kicked the tree with a prayer three times, "Why have you hidden all these idols in your branches without letting me know. I curse you and you must die now." It took me 2 hours to chase all those spirits away from my old friend because he used to spell the black magic, mediums, and witchcraft onto other people. However, a few days after that, the tree began to dry from the top down to the root and completely died about a month later.

Five months later, the tree was blown down by a storm. While we were burning all the paper boxes, objects, incenses, and other materials for my old friend, other people and I saw that the heavy smoke from the fire turned into 3 persons who were walking inside the fence of my old friend's home. I used a water hose to spray the water onto the smoke and suddenly, those three persons jumped across the fence to the neighbor's side of yard, then slowly rose into the sky and disappeared. Since that day, he has been healthy and no more sickness again. Now, we know that demons always stay with idols and religious materials and objects such as cross, picture of famous people, kings, queens, and movie stars who are alive and deceased. Some people even burn incense and worship the pictures of the king of Thailand, queen of England and many other famous people even they are still alive today. Their actions bring sickness, illness, and other problems into themselves.

Demon Spirit Slept with a Young Lady

In 2005, a young lady went to Mexico for a vacation for a week, then came home with some nice posters and she put them in her bedroom. Then, she saw a handsome big and tall gentle man came and slept with her in her bed every night. The man went away in morning without talking and doing anything to her. She saw any person there with her, she knew for sure that she locked her bedroom door every night, but he came in the room every night for weeks without problems. She, then was afraid of the man and no longer dare to sleep in her own room. She went and slept in her parents' room. Her father, then called me to pray for her. I asked her about any spiritual objects and materials that she might have, but she said that she did not have any such things in her room. We, then went into her room and prayed for her.

Suddenly, I felt some strange things in the room, then I searched around the room and found some posters in her room. I looked at those posters and saw that the eyes of one of the posters were kind of moving back and forth. The eyes of that picture of that posters were moving when my eyes moved, but when my eyes stopped, they stopped, too. I told everyone that the demons were in the picture of that poster. The demons, spirits, sickness, and cancers are the same. I asked for permission to burn that poster and she let me do it. I burned the poster in fire and prayed for her, then her room has been quiet, and she has been sleeping in peace in that room until today.

Another Cancer Healed

In 2008, I had a pastor friend who lived about 100 miles away from me. We didn't talk to each other for about a year. One day, he called me and asked for healing prayer. I asked him to see what was wrong with him and he said that he had cancer. His doctors could not find the cancer until a few days ago and it was too late already. His doctors told him that he had only a few more weeks to live. He was so weak and could no longer stand up.

I prayed for him and suddenly, the Holy Spirit revealed to me that he had some demonic materials in his possession. I called him and told him accordingly. He told me that he had been a pastor for years but had not known about this and did something terribly wrong recently. He filed a lawsuit in court against his former boss after his former boss fired him from his job without any reasons. He won and his former boss was arrested and put in the jail. His former boss had to post a bail of $1 million dollars for his release. His former boss' court case was still ongoing in court for another year or two. All the lawsuit paperwork was still in his home. I told him that, that was the problem. I requested that he, please throw all of the paperwork in fire, burn them and forget all about the case in court because he was a pastor. He should not involve in any kind of court cases or suing anybody.

The Bible said that if someone slap you on the right cheek turn your left also. The pastor asked what about the court appointments and I told him that you needed to forget about them and the whole incident, too, then the court will dismiss the case, and your former boss could go free. After that Jesus Christ would forgive you and heal you from your cancer. The pastor did according to my advice and was able to eat some foods on the following day. The pastor was also able to drive, shop and go everywhere he wanted to go.

Today, the pastor is still living and serves Jesus Christ as a pastor. A lot of other pastors do not practice the word of God and face some kind of consequences in life. Now we know that if we possess something against God and not according to God's will, the evil spirits will jump in to take control of the situation, and the problem get worse to worst. Thus, we need to forgive others before we can receive a real forgiveness for ourselves. It's a very simple way to just forgive others and don't have to find any special medicine to treat the cancer and other diseases. The Lord Jesus Christ will heal us.

Healing a Lady with Rhino Horn and Mental Illness

In early 2009, a friend of mine called me that Chai Waa was a 65-year-old lady who had mental illness and needed my prayer. I knew that I could not help her, but my Lord God could heal her from the craziest spirit. I, then prayed for her and she was healed. Since then, she has been going to my church with her family. Her daughter, Muang Lin told me that the shamans did their best for her, but could not heal her after hundreds of chickens, more than ten pigs and many cows were sacrificed to her family spirits. Her family, then called me to pray for her. I did and she was healed. After she was healed, she told me later that she also went to many churches for prayers and every of them did, but none of them could get her healed.

In fact, as soon as my team and I sang songs and prayed for her, she cried out, "Where are we going to stay? Where are going to hide? They are attacking us like fire!" We knew at that moment that our joint prayer was working. So, we kept on praying with a command and loud voice, then she shouted, "We have nowhere to hide. We need to run! Let's run!" Suddenly, she fell to the ground for a moment, then was healed, got up, and communicated with us normally. We, then went home and thought that she would be healed forever, but at the middle of that night, her daughter called me again that her mother's mental illness came back and she was manic again as before.

She requested that I went to her and pray for her again. My prayer team and I had to drive an hour to her home and prayed for her again, but this time, our prayers did not work at the beginning. We had to read the Scripture in **Mark 16: 15-19** and **Ephesians 6:10-20,** burn about a truck load of her belongings such as old clothes, antiques, and other possession, then prayed for her again before she was healed. A few days after this second prayer and healing, her daughter called again that her mother was sick again with the same insanity and needed our prayer again.

My prayer team and I hurriedly went to her home again. When we got there, we complained that we were so tired, our families were so tired, and our congregation was also so tired, too. Everyone was about to give up, but we prayed again, "In the name of the Lord, why don't you, the evil spirits go out of this lady now?" She answered, "I need my Rhino Horn. I won't leave until I get my Rhino Horn!" Her family searched to their best and found the Rhino Horn. We burned it, then prayed again, **"In the name of the Lord, the Living**

God, above all gods, we command you, the evil spirits go out of this lady now! Now! Now!" Suddenly, she fell on the ground, got up, and was healed.

Her mental illness was healed for good. She told me later that her late husband dedicated the Rhino Horns to the evil spirit, then told people that it was a sacred horn for healing and he earned some money from it. The Rhino Horn itself had nothing to do with illness, but because people burned incense and worship it as an idol. That's why it was possessed by the evil spirits and the evil spirits caused the illnesses. Demons always come into clothing's, posters, cross, and so on that people used for worshipping spirits. In Israel, some people make the pictures of Jesus, Mary, and Moses into little cross and other things that are like idols and sell them on the streets and stores. The non-Christians burn incense and bow down to them as idols. Some Christians buy those items and keep them, too. The spirits in those items go into the bodies of those keepers and make them sick and ill. Thus, in order for them to get well, they have to destroy and burn all of those items away (**Judges 2:6-23**).

Empty Wheelchair for Older Man

Right, Mr. Chiamfinh Ta was able to stand up from his wheelchair by power of God. Center, Paul Seng Chao was praying, and left Oufin pushed wheelchair to church.

Mr. Chiemfinh Ta was a non-believer who lived with his non-believer son for a long time. He was sick, could not walk, and had to be pushed in a wheelchair for many years. His non-believer son worshipped all the spirits for him without him being healed. Both his son and he exhausted all means in their old religion, then let him accept the Lord Jesus Chris and see if it might help. He moved to his younger son and accepted Jesus Christ to be his Lord like his younger son, U-Fin, then he was healed, but still could not walk. One day he felt the power of the Holy Spirit was upon him while he was listening to my preaching about the Holy Spirit, Jesus Christ, and God, then he stood up in the middle of the service and began walking around the church. He even walked home that day and has never used the wheelchair again His name is Chiamfin Ta Saelee. He is 71 years old.

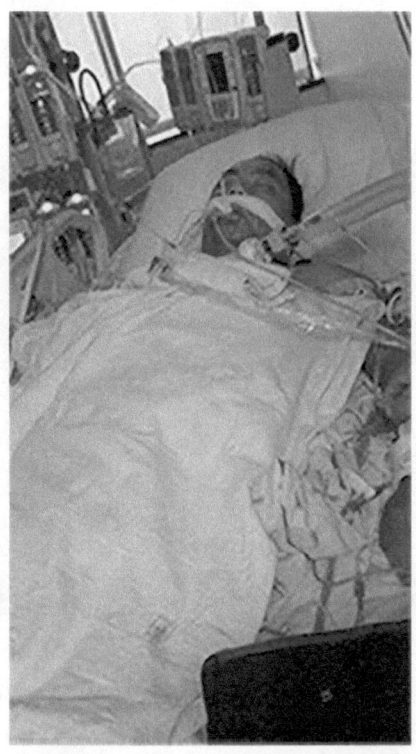

Mr. Ou Seng Saechao who was rushed to an emergency room of a hospital in Salem, Oregon due to his heart attack and four artery blockades. He also had multiple problems with stroke, high blood pressure, and sugar in the blood. He was transferred to Kaiser Sunnyside Hospital in Clackamas County, Oregon later that month. The doctors there reported that he needed a bi-pass surgery to survive, but they could not guarantee that he would regain his consciousness after the surgery. He might even die during the surgery because his heart was too weak. In case if he denied a surgery, he would die within about three months.

However, he decided not to go through the surgery and called me to pray for him. After prayer in 2012, he was healed and has been healthy ever since.

Mr. Ou fin Saelee was healed from brain tumor and stomach cancer. Today, he is in good health and serving God and God's child in Sacramento, CA.

Mr. Ou fin Saelee who was rushed to Stockton Hospital for treatments of his stomach cancer and brain tumor. He was unable to eat anything for many days at home and many weeks at the hospital, but by the power of God he did not have to go through a surgery and chemotherapy, but prayers only, then he was healed and has been living healthy since 2012.

A 4 year old girl who see spirits.

A little girl was always fighting with a spirit girl over her toys. She said to the spirit, "You don't take my toys, why do you always take my toys?" Her parents looked around but didn't see anyone. Her parents ask her, "Who do you fight with?" She said, "there is a girl here always playing with my toys. I don't like her." Her parents ask her, "what does she look like?" She described the spirit girl as 'a little girl like me'. Then the parents asked my prayer group & I to pray. We then sanctify the house with olive oil and cleansed the house, then the spirit left. Now, parents asked her, "where is the girl that was always playing with your toys?" She said the girl went through the front door and disappeared.

A man healed from seizure

In 2014, a man was diagnosed with seizure who also was a smoker, came to us asking for help. He took medication for years, but nothing seemed to help. One day, he came and asked for pray. My prayer group came together and prayed. Suddenly, his 7-year-old son saw 15 spirits leaving his dad. He felt something lift from his shoulder, his body felt light. He stopped smoking and was healed from his seizure that day. Today he is total healed.

My testimonies of blessings

One night, I was making noodles and didn't have any lemons left. It's not worth to go the store for one lemon, however I needed it. I thought in my heart, how can I get a lemon. Half an hour passed, the doorbell rang. I opened the door, and a lady stood there with two bags of lemons. She said, "Someone gave it to me, and I want give to you." She left without coming in the house. And I didn't recognize her. God will provide all our needs for those who believe in Him.

In addition, I have planted bamboo shoots in my back yard but is not the season to harvest yet. I looked around the bamboo area. I keep wondering where I can get some fresh bamboo for dinner. Suddenly, my phone rang. The other end of the receiver said, "Pastor, do you like bamboo shoot?" I replied, "Yes, but where can I get some?"

She said, "Don't worry just wait at home. Someone will drop off two packs of fresh bamboo shoot to you from Fresno, Ca." I keep thanking the Lord and His mercy endures forever.

One morning, I am alone at home and wanted to eat Vietnamese noodle. Keep thinking for about one hour and then the phone ring. I picked up the phone, the receiver said, "Do you like to eat Vietnamese noodle soup?" I said, "Yes." He said to go to the restaurant at 11:AM. It will be my treat. I proceeded to go the restaurant. This person spoke to the owner and requested, when this pastor comes here every time just send the bill to me. I go there very often, and the bill is paid. We both went back for lunch, and I said, "this time, I will pay for the meal." After we ate, when it was time to pay the bill, I went to counter and the cashier told me, "Your table has already been paid for." I asked, "who paid for it?" She pointed to one table in the back, and a man waved his hand to me and said "bye." All I can say is thank you, my Lord and My God. He is good and endures forever.

One summer's day, it felt like 100 degrees outside. I needed to drink some cold sweet drink. I wanted a Vietnamese dessert drink called three color drink. I didn't mention it to anyone but kept thinking inside my heart. By now, it's time to have prayer. A lady walked in the church with a three-color drink and thought to herself this is not enough for everybody so I will give to you pastor. Do you want it? I said yes that's what my heart desire. The smallest gesture goes a long way. God cares about our life. God is so good, and He is good all the time.

One time, I need hair cut but I need Christian salon to cut my hair. But don't know any. I think for two days, then phone call, other end said do you like hair cut? I said yes, I do. He said, please come pick up me then we go to a Christian lady for hair cut for you and me. I did, then we went to salon center, there is a Hmong Christian lady.

She is very nice and professional. He said to lady, every time pastor need hair cut just bill to me. Phil 4:19. 2Cor 9:8 He is awesome God.

The Church

How Paul Seng Ministries church began. The deacons came together and discussed that we no longer wanted to rent peoples' place for Sunday service to worship our God and Jesus Christ. We all wanted to buy a piece of land and build a church building of our own. We found a piece of land listed for $115,000, but our church had only $30,000 in our church account. We made an offer to pay $100,000 dollars cash to the seller and our offer was accepted. We signed the offer to pay cash in full. As the closing date near, I couldn't sleep because my mind kept on pondering for ways to get the $100,000 dollars which was needed. I continually prayed day and night. A couple of weeks after my prayer, our church donated up to $40,000.

This time, my brother-in-law saw that I was worried about the funds. And he donated $20,000 dollars to our church for buying the land. Now, we still needed $10,000 more to pay off the land at the closing. We were at the wit's end and asked the seller to carry a contract of $10,000 without interest for 90 days and we would pay him off. The seller agreed with the term, and the escrow closed. Only a few weeks after the closing, we went to the bank and found that our bank account balance was already more than the $10,000 we needed. We, then paid off the land without having to carry the contract. After paying off the land, we still have over $10,000 in our church bank account. Now, we knew that all our prayers were answered through miracles from God. Two years after paying off the land, we filed for a permit to build our church building, but 32 families in that neighborhood filed a petition against the plan and the government could not approve our request for building the church building on the land. So, we had to list the land for sale and sold it for $180,000.

We took the money and bought another piece of much better land for $130,000 and we still had $50,000 cash in our church bank account balance. We filed for a permit to build our church building on the land for the second time. Again, our request was denied by the county because our land and that surrounding area were for oil drilling. We had to sell this second piece of land, and we sold it for $430,000.

We, then bought a third piece of bigger and better land for $220,000 dollars cash. We filed for a permit to build our church building for the third time. This time, the county denied our permit request because county already had a plan to put a new street through the land. We had to sell our third piece of land, and we sold it for $400,000.

Now we have enough money to buy a complete church building. In 2006, we bought our current church building and land from another congregation for $715,000 dollars. Now, we no longer had to file for any kind of permits, but we found later that the seller did not finish so many things inside and outside of the building and the land. The parking lot and a big ditch in front of the building were not complete.

We needed at least 250 truckloads of dirt to fill the ditch, but we did not have $20,000 dollars to buy the dirt. We, then prayed to God for the needed money to buy the dirt. After our consistence prayers, a man walked by our church and saw our empty ditch, then asked me, "Do you need the dirt?" I answered, "Yes, how much?" He answered, "It's free." He, then transported all of the 250 truckloads of dirt to us without charging us. Now, we needed a tractor to move the dirt to fill the ditch, but we did not have about $10,000 dollars to rent one. I prayed to God again for help.

This time a man came and asked me to rent a space to him for putting his tractor for few months. I said to him that if he let us use it for moving the dirt to fill the ditch, then we would not charge him, but let him store it in our parking lot for free. He was so happy and accepted the term. We used the tractor to finish filling our ditch without having to pay any money. We were so grateful for God's help of sending the man and his tractor to us.

Three months later, the man came and drove his tractor away with happiness. Now, we still needed to expand our parking lots to accommodate our growing church members, but we did not have about $80,000 to expand the needed 45 more parking spaces. I prayed again to God for help for the fourth project.

This time, all our church members volunteered their labor, donated concrete, paid for the mixing and dropping of the concrete. Finally, our parking lot was done for only $14,000 instead $80,000. Our church's building is 4,620 square feet on 2.11 acres of land. We are so grateful for God's mercy and blessing from the past to presence and into the future.

Church Building

This is a photo of my wife dressed up in our Mien or Yao costume in front of our church during our Easter celebration of Jesus Christ in 2012. Like all marriage couples, we have good times and bad times. We have been blessed in our marriage for 38years. God has blessed us with 2 sons, one daughter, 3 grandsons, and 2 grand-daughters

The parking lot need to pave for 50 cars to park. The church does not have money. The cost about $80k to finish. I pray to God then some one said to me. I will donate the concrete, but you do the labor then I agree. So, we finish the parking lot. Now front fence, it needs $10k to finish and church don't have money, I keep for 2 days while I still praying a guy came start to clear the way for fence. I ask what are doing? He answers, I got money for fence, so finish the fence. Now all done, next, I think want to kill a cow to celebrate Jesus for thank giving. But no money, where can I get money, couple days later, a guy call from out of state, he said pastor do you think to celebrate thanksgiving to God is good idea? Of course I said. He continues ok then I will send you a check just buy a big cow such day I will be there, we can celebrate for the feast, good its cool. We did get cow and celebrate Jesus, enjoy on celebrate day. Now it came to easter day close by few months, I think who will be donate a cow for easter for resurrection day for the lord God. Then few days some one call me, hey paster the easter days is near can we kill the cow like last time. Yes, I said whatever good for the lord God it is good idea. The same guy buys a big cow to celebrate for easter not just cow but 20 chicken. We done this on so many years, I think, why we change from cow to deer or buffalo. Then somebody call me. Pastor, can we get buffalo for this thanksgiving? I said yes, but where can we get it. he said I know a place can get one. Only need to approve it. I said good idea. Then we did it got cow, buffalo, deer, now we are cow number 37 cows. Some time we ask for pheasant, chicken. Or quail.

Pictured here is my grandson Anthony Saechao, and to the right is Nai Saeleee dressed in old costume clothes. They both receive Jesus Christ as Savior. The second generation to call on the Name of Jesus Christ the Messiah the Savior in America.

Below is the town, I came from at Huei Kunbong village, Tonperng District, Bokeo province of Laos in 2008. The bamboo house, the village, animals and people live together in the country side. I just show my children where we came from and how much God bless us today.

We are live in United States of America do not understand other world. People live in darkness and always possessed by spirits. Because they worship the natures. Num 25:1-3

Time Frame

My life, since I was born always migration from place to places until refugee to Thailand. My family and I landed in Seattle, Washington, U.S.A in 1980, then accepted the Lord Jesus Christ in 1982 during the time my wife was so sick with low blood pressure, and I was having migraine headache. I had to leave my job and moved to a warmer climate in California where my sister and I were searching for God. Later we found the healing power through the Holy Spirit and all our health problems were healed. Now we know that God loves my wife and I. That's why God used our sickness to move us to Sacramento, California. Or I might still fooling around with my many alcohol drinking friends and would not know about the power of the Holy Spirit and don't know how to serve the Lord God, either knew how to ask the wisdom of God but confuse so huge day by days, we made a lot mistake but mercy of God still guide through those years, final we found the answer in Jesus alone.

We started our church at Sacramento Unity Church in 1992. The pastor of this church had some personal problems and left the church at the end of 1994 without telling anyone. His left behind congregation was lost and dysfunctional. I had to responsible for our whole ministries from 1995 on. I, then was called by God to quit my other full-time job to serve God in our ministries full time. In 1997, we started forming a non-profit organization and changed our church name from Sacramento Unity to Calvary Christian Church.

From 1997 to 2006 we were unable to get things done within ministries and prayed to God for guidance. In 2008, God answered our prayers, and we were making good progress. We, then changed our church name from the Calvary Christian to Paul Seng Ministries. Our prayer team always pray for the discernment from the Holy Spirit to guide us in our daily life. I must depend on God to guide me and my church every second. Otherwise, we cannot over the demonic spirits which aim at stealing, killing and destroying us and other Christians around the world.

Left Fay Chao was healed from prolong illness, low blood pressure and right, daughter in-law was heal from fearfulness, and unable to sleep but by the power of God. Today she's live a happy life with daughter Anyla Saechao is dress in old costumes.

I told my children where we came from a very poor country like hell and God lift my family from hell to heaven, now we are facing to go the heaven in name of Jesus Christ by his mercy and love of the father that gave his only Son Jesus Christ and show the way to heaven. Below is our costumes clothes to show our children and grandchildren who we are and where we came from.

My special thanks go to the government of the United States of America and the United Nations for saving the lost peoples around the world like me, my family and friends through the Lord Jesus Christ the Savior. May God bless the United States of America and United Nations with a long-lasting prosperity. Our congregation will continue to pray for America and good ministries into the world. May God bless America forever.

Pastor Dawin Cranor, Paul Seng Chao, Fay Chao dress in Lao clothes.

Paul Seng Ministries
9019 Alder Ave
Sacramento Ca, 95829

Editor's Remark:

I, Pastor Seng Fo Chao spent 55 hours on editing this testimonial booklet for Pastor Paul Seng Chao from July 10, 2014, to August 02, 2014, because I love God and God's People around the world. I believe and pray that this testimonial booklet will lead a lot of people into Jesus Christ our Lord. May God bless Pastor Paul Seng Chao, Paul Seng Ministries, New Life in Christ Church, United Christians Oversea Mission, the U.S and the whole world, Amen.

I would like to thank you for Rev Sengfo Chao, my Daughter Cindy Saechao and my niece, Lisa Medina, Chang Saeteurn, Pastor Dawin Cranor, Dr Michael Catopino, Cleavelence Jones, David and Grace Lue and all our prayers team for their help edited the book. May God bless you and continue prosperous every area in your family business.

Praise the God and Father of our Lord Jesus Christ. Through Christ, God has blessed us with every spiritual blessing that heaven has to offer. Eph 1:3

Hear, O Israel: The LORD our God is one LORD: And thou shalt love the LORD thy God with all thine heart, and with all thy soul, and with all thy might. Deu 6:4-5.

In this world there is only one God, but human made too many gods and too much Chaos, but Jesus Christ is the Messiah the only solution to the answer. John 14:6

www.ingramcontent.com/pod-product-compliance
Lightning Source LLC
LaVergne TN
LVHW041538060526
838200LV00037B/1033